THE
CONQUEST OF THE
MIND

BY ELBERT WILLIS

FILL THE GAP PUBLICATIONS
P. O. BOX 30760
LAFAYETTE, LOUISIANA 70503

ISBN: 0-89858-037-4
First Printing, August, 1980
Second Printing, August, 1982

CONTENTS

CONQUEST OF THE MIND
INTRODUCTION

When an individual receives Jesus and is born again of the Spirit of God, he instantaneously becomes a new creature in Christ. His spirit is reborn and God comes and tabernacles Himself in that person's spirit in the form of the Holy Spirit. From that moment forth that person is a Christian. His spirit is totally saved and he is redeemed. However, even though he has been born again, the body and the mind can still be out of line with the Word of God. You can love the Lord Jesus with all of your heart and still have a sick body, a frustrated mind, and be unable to walk in total victory in every area of life if your mind is not renewed by the Word. There is no defeat in Jesus, He is the Conqueror and the Overcomer, and He says we are born of Him. Therefore, through inheritance from our spiritual birth rights, we are also conquerors and overcomers in Christ Jesus. We have natural birth rights from our earthly parents, but we also have birth rights from our heavenly Father. What we need to do is to learn more about the birth rights from our heavenly Father and begin to live in that realm, because being limited to the natural realm will continuously bring defeat.

What we are saying is that salvation is instant, but conquest of the mind is progressive, and is also the key to receiving revelation from the Word through the Holy Spirit, which must be translated into action on our part that God might be glorified. John 16:13 says, "HOWBEIT WHEN HE, THE SPIRIT OF TRUTH, IS COME, HE WILL GUIDE YOU INTO ALL TRUTH." The Holy Spirit is the Spirit of Truth, and He has come to dwell within you and me, to reveal the Word unto us

1

Revelation is simply a transfer of knowledge from the spirit to the mind. If your mind is continually controlled by Satan through fear, frustration, worry, confusion, disappointment, resentment, bitterness, etc., the Holy Spirit is unable to transfer the knowledge of God to your mind. Therefore, your mind must be conquered by the Holy Spirit of God. Your mind must be reprogrammed by the Word of God so that when the Holy Spirit of God inside of you speaks, you will have the knowledge of the Word in your mind, and then you can understand what He is telling you to do. God wants you to have this revelation from the Holy Spirit within. He wants it to come to your mind so you will know how to act and talk in order that Jesus may be glorified.

The mind is like a computer. A computer is programmed until it has a certain amount of information in it. Ever since we were born, the devil (the god of this world) has been programming our minds. The Bible says in James 4:4, "THE FRIENDSHIP OF THE WORLD IS ENMITY WITH GOD." This means that much of our programming done by the world was from Satan himself. When you begin to see the truths of the Bible, which are from another world, another dimension, and another Being, they do not line up with the thoughts that have been fed into your mind by this world. Because of this, the first thing you say of the Bible is, "Myth, folklore, imagination,"and your computer rejects it. Your mind cannot understand how waters can part. It cannot understand that it is possible to walk on water; how you can simply lay hands on the sick and say, "Be healed, in the Name of Jesus," and they recover; how you can speak in a strange language that you have not learned and yet you are speaking to God. Your natural computer cannot understand how the dead can be raised or how you could even have two births. That computer of yours has been programmed by the world, and when you begin trying to put heavenly information into it, it fights. The devil has planned it that way because he doesn't want you to accept the truth, the Word of God.

When I first heard of "speaking in tongues" my computer kicked it out. I said, "That's of the devil." I thought it was ri-

2

diculous the first time I went to a charismatic meeting and saw people raising their hands. I didn't go to college and graduate from the New Orleans Baptist Seminary to raise my hands! According to my past programming that was not to be done in church because it was irreverent. It is the same with clapping and shouting in church; I had been programmed against it. The first F.G.B.M.F.I. convention I went to was in Denver, Colorado. I saw arms and legs growing out, and people were taking off their glasses because their eyes had been healed. My computer said, "How much are they paying them? What kind of trick is this?" It is for the same reason (lack of mind renewal) that people today are having such difficulty understanding the Word of God. They have been programmed by the world. The best thing to do is to find out what the world tells you to do, turn around and go the opposite direction. You will be closer to God. That is a key to go by until the mind is reprogrammed by the Word. Until the mind is reprogrammed with God's language, which is His Word, you will not be able to understand what He is talking about when He speaks to you because your mind is too occupied with the language of the world. You will want to rebuke the devil because what God speaks is usually contrary to your natural way of thinking.

Remember, the new birth comes instantly, but the progressive education, retraining and reprogramming of the mind must be done by the Word of God. You must erase the old and put in the new. The old mind is filled with fear. It has been programmed to fuss back if someone started fussing at you. When your mind becomes renewed and someone starts fussing at you, you can say, "Praise the Lord!" What has happened is a reprogramming. God desires to continue this education program, and the Word and Spirit of God are the teachers. The Word of God is a new subject to a newly born child of God. If you were to go to college and start taking any new subject, you would be given a new book because you wouldn't know anything about the subject at that point. When you begin to learn the basis of it, you are laying a foundation and you can then understand that particular subject. The Word of God is a subject

3

from another world which the natural mind cannot perceive. This is why the natural man rejects the Word of God. They reject miracles because they cannot understand them. It is easy for me to understand miracles now, but I did not understand miracles ten years ago. My mind has been reprogrammed. Before it was renewed I could not conceive dancing, unless it was in a club. Now I can easily conceive dancing in the house of the Lord because I know what the Word of God says concerning it. I found out that it is right to praise the Lord, but it has to be translated into action to glorify God. God's love, joy, peace, faith, anointing and victory dwell inside of you in the presence of the Holy Spirit of God. God wants His Holy Spirit (heavenly knowledge inside of you) to control your mind so you can begin to act like Jesus down here. Remember, you will not act like the rest of the world. You are not supposed to be like them. You have been born twice, and when you die you are going to another place. How can you still act like them? If you act like them you are forcing your old nature to reign and rule in your life. I don't act like the other people out there, and they look at me like I am the one who is backwards. On the contrary, anyone who does not accept Jesus Christ as Lord is backwards, no matter how smart they are intellectually. They can be intellectual giants and at the same time be spiritually illiterate. It is my desire that your mind become reprogrammed by the Word of God.

Elbert Willis

OUTLINE ... CHAPTER ONE
Marks of an Improper Foundation

Salvation is instant **but** conquest of the mind is progressive. **The key** to receiving revelations from Holy Spirit and to be translated into action to glorify God, is to conquer the mind and bring it under the control of the Word of God.

I. **WRONG MOTIVES:** Produce wrong action that exposes roots. Mt. 6:33 "Seek ye first the kingdom of God and His righteousness and all these things shall be added unto you."

Key thoughts:
*   Desire to have "things" - overrides Word that requires foundation.
*   Lust for benefits is revealed in no preparation.
*   Unwillingness to pay the cost to establish reception foundation discloses roots of insincerity - laziness - lust.

II. **CONFORMITY:** Rom. 12:2 "Be not conformed to this world"

1. **"BE NOT"** Present imperative verb that forbids the continuance of an action already going on -- requires an immediate shift in directions - a warning of the result of a continuation of direction.

    Plea of an all knowing God to His beloved children who don't know.

2. **"CONFORMED"** Outward expression that does not come from within, nor represent Holy Spirit.
   - Patterned after some definite thing.
   - Expression formed from position without Christ.
   - Masquerading in the mannerisms, speech, expressions, styles, habits of this world which you no longer represent.
3. **"TO THIS WORLD"** Spirit of the age: Floating mass of thoughts, opinions, speculations, hopes, impulses, aims, aspirations, current in the world at any time, which it may be impossible to accurately define, yet it constitutes an effective power of influences.

III. **CONFUSION:** II Thess. 2:2 "That ye be not soon shaken in mind and troubled in spirit, word, nor letter as from us."

Key thoughts:
* Warns against mental agitation, disturbance of poise, off balance or swayed by senses.
* Points to outside force causing rocking motion as: building by earthquake, ship by storm or ship blown away because insecurely anchored, but to be controlled by a mind enlightened by revelation of God's Word.

IV. **FALLING:** Heb. 12:3 "Be wearied and faint in your minds."

1. **"FAINT IN YOUR MINDS"** Reverse of vigor - cheerful. When faith is not operative we are left to cope with situation with power of natural mind which cannot stand pressure of enemy.
2. **"WEARY"** Exhausted - despondent - sinking of spirit through power of difficulty and opposition.

Result is: Partial or complete abandonment of vows and stand.

V.   TALKATIVENESS: Prov. 29:11 "a fool uttereth all his mind, but a wise man keepeth it in till afterwards."
1.   Untrained mind will spit forth: Bad confessions, gossip - foolish things - irrelevant things.
2.   Can be hidden often but pressure reveals.

VI. INSTABILITY: Ja. 1:8 "A doubleminded man is unstable in all his ways." Unsteady - fickle - wobbles - reels as drunk, or cork on water to shore and away - cannot choose decisively.
     Two results: (God made the rules)
1.   Disqualifies himself from much. Ja. 1:7 "Let not that man think he shall receive anything of the Lord."
2.   Hypocrisy or abandonment.

VII. MISDIRECTION: Eph. 4:17 "Walk not as other Gentiles walk, in the vanity of their mind."
1.   "WALK NOT" Conduct or order one's behavior in direction of heathen's - Walks after same things - Mt. 6:33 "added."
2.   "VANITY OF MIND" That which is aimless, resultless, futile except in mind of ungodly - void of real worth - beckoning of fantasy which appears to be real and satisfying, of value but upon reception has no satisfying influence.
     Gal. 3:1 "O foolish Galatians, who hath bewitched you, that ye should not obey the truth (Word)." Mt. 6:33; Rom. 12:2; II Thess. 2:2; Heb. 12:3; Prov. 29:11; Ja. 1:8; Eph. 4:17.

CHAPTER ONE
Marks of an Improper Foundation

In this chapter we are going to look at some **MARKS OF AN IMPROPER FOUNDATION.** If any one of these fits your life, that is where you will want to start working. It is possible that all of them will fit you in some area. We desire to help you locate yourself, so that you will know where to work. You must find out where your problem is, in your walk with Jesus, before you can correct it.

I. **WRONG MOTIVES** is one of the first marks of an improper foundation in an unrenewed mind. Wrong motives produce wrong actions which expose roots. Matthew 6:33 says, "SEEK YE FIRST THE KINGDOM OF GOD AND HIS RIGHTEOUSNESS AND ALL THESE THINGS SHALL BE ADDED UNTO YOU." Desire to have "things" overrides the Word, which requires you to have a proper foundation. Unwillingness to pay the costs to establish a receptive foundation discloses roots of insecurity, laziness, and even lust.

The things God is speaking of in Matthew 6:33 are the things that the heathen seek after. The Gentile, the lost man, seeks after cars, homes, clothes, etc. God says that if you will seek Him first, He will give those things to you. He says in Mark 11:24, "THEREFORE I SAY UNTO YOU, WHAT THINGS SOEVER YE DESIRE, WHEN YE PRAY, BELIEVE THAT YE RECEIVE THEM, AND YE SHALL HAVE THEM." He says in Matthew 21:22, "AND ALL THINGS, WHATSOEVER YE SHALL ASK IN PRAYER, BELIEVING, YE

SHALL RECEIVE." What happens many times when a mind has not been renewed by the Word of God, is that one comes to God and hears the faith and victorious, abundant life teachings and begins to key in on all these things. He begins praying and claiming the things of the world and does not spend the proper time to prepare himself by getting his mind renewed. That exposes a root that should not be there.

The desire to have things overrides the Word. Too many Christians are trying to do many things with their natural ability and strength. " . . . RECKON YE ALSO YOURSELVES TO BE DEAD '. . ." (Romans 6:11). "NOT I BUT CHRIST LIVETH IN ME . . ." (Galatians 2:20). JESUS IS THE VINE AND I AM THE BRANCH. WITHOUT HIM I CAN DO NOTHING. (John 15:5) Praise God, we are not without Him; however, if you are seeking things, you will not take the time to learn the Word. If you are trying to get a new car and at the same time you are not settling down to learn the Word, you have a root there. If you are saying, "Father God, I want a new home," but you are not preparing yourself by getting your mind renewed, you are exposing roots by a lack of preparation. If this is the case, it is things that you are after, because the Word says, "SEEK YE FIRST THE KINGDOM OF GOD AND HIS RIGHTEOUSNESS AND ALL THESE THINGS SHALL BE ADDED UNTO YOU." Most people's minds cannot comprehend that, because they have been told all their lives that one has to work, strain and sweat to get anything. The world has told us all our lives that you have to be shrewd, smart and wise to get it. God says, "SEEK ME FIRST AND I WILL GIVE IT TO YOU." The mind cannot comprehend that. God says that if you want to have all the things of the world that everyone sweats, strains and craves for, just forget about them and seek Him first, and He will just give them to you. It takes a renewed mind to comprehend that.

Lust for benefits is revealed in no preparation. If you are trying to get God to save your loved one, heal your body, pay your bills off and protect you, and you're not laying your foundation by preparing yourself in the Word, lust is being revealed in your life. You are trying to get something from God without paying the cost. In II TIMOTHY 2:15 God says, STUDY TO SHOW THYSELF APPROVED UNTO GOD, A WORKMAN THAT NEEDETH NOT TO BE ASHAMED, RIGHTLY DIVIDING THE WORD OF TRUTH." This is the way you learn how to receive from God. Unwillingness to pay the cost to establish a receptive foundation discloses roots of insincerity and laziness. Many people want all the benefits God promises, but they do not want to do much studying. They won't even go to hear a teaching once or twice a week because they feel they already have enough. It is obvious that they do not have much, by simply observing their lives. The mind must be renewed. If you do not take the time to study and meditate in the Word, it shows your insincerity. You are trying to manipulate God. God has laid down the rules and regulations, and you must learn the Word in order to receive from Him.

If you are unable to walk in victory spiritually, physically, mentally or financially, you have an improper foundation in that particular area. What we are trying to do is to help you to see where your foundation is weak or cracked, so that you can patch it. Sometimes, you will find out there is no foundation there at all. With the Word of God a foundation can be built. We must be willing to be honest with ourselves and we must be willing to spend the time, to pay the price, to build a proper foundation by God's Word.

II.   CONFORMITY is another mark of an improper foundation that will keep you from bringing you mind under the control of the Spirit of God.

1.   "BE NOT" — Romans 12:2 says, and BE NOT CONFORMED TO THIS WORLD . . ." It says, "BE NOT." This is a present, imperative verb that forbids the continuance of an action already going on. What does God mean by telling us to stop doing this action? First of all, He knows what you are worth. He saved you. Your mind was programmed by the world. He knows what you have been taught, how you have been talking, how you have been walking, and how you are living. He also knows what you are going to be doing after you get saved if your mind is not renewed. For example, II Timo-

11

thy 1:7 says, "FOR GOD HAS NOT GIVEN US THE SPIRIT OF FEAR; BUT OF POWER, AND OF LOVE, AND OF A SOUND MIND." How many Christians remain in fear after they have been saved? God says that fear is not of Him, but of the devil. It is the same as with cursing. You quit cursing, but you didn't quit being afraid, because you were taught all your life that it is proper to be fearful. God forbids you to continue in that kind of life. He says, "I didn't give you that fear." Do you realize what God is saying? He is saying, "Son, I forbid you to keep on being afraid. I have something better for you. I forbid you to keep on being resentful, hurt, depressed, lonely and frustrated. I have something better for you." He has love, joy, peace, etc. Thank God that he forbids us to do those things.

2. "CONFORMED." If you were driving down the road and an officer walked in front of your car and said to stop, I believe you would stop. It would be for your benefit. Now, if you don't stop you are going to pay the price. God says to ". . . BE NOT CONFORMED TO THIS WORLD." If you don't stop conforming to this world, you are going to pay the price. Your mind is never going to be renewed. It requires an immediate shift of direction. You have been trained all your life to do something, and when you read the Bible it tells you something else. Jesus said in Matthew 5:39 that ". . .WHOSOEVER SHALL SMITE THEE ON THY RIGHT CHEEK, TURN TO HIM THE OTHER ALSO." All your life you have been told to hit back. All your life you have been taught to worry, when Jesus repeatedly said to "TAKE NO THOUGHT." You have been taught to go to the doctor and get medicine. The Word of God says, "IS ANY SICK AMONG YOU?" LET HIM CALL FOR THE ELDERS OF THE CHURCH; AND LET THEM PRAY OVER HIM, ANOINTING HIM WITH OIL IN THE NAME OF THE LORD; AND THE PRAYER OF FAITH SHALL SAVE (heal) THE SICK . . ." (James 5:14-15.) The natural mind says, "He cannot mean that. He means that if any among you is sick, let him call the doctor." That is what the world and its system says. The world says that the way to get ahead is to skimp, work and strain. The Words says that riches and wealth are the gift of God (Ecclesiastes 5:19). There

are Christians who are saved and filled with the Holy Spirit who will not obey the Word of God, and they are trying to get everything the world's way. God has a better way for you. His way is a whole new system that supersedes the world's system. Their system will never match God's system for you. A warning of the result of a continuation of direction is " . . . BE NOT CONFORMED TO THIS WORLD . . . " What He is saying is to stop. Quit talking and acting like the unrenewed man. You are going in the wrong direction. What He is saying is that in the past it was all right to conform because you were lost. You are now Hi servant; don't go that way anymore. He is warning you of what is ahead. You have the door open for the devil if you are disobeying the Word of God. All your life you have been taught by the world to think one way. Now the Word of God is showing you the true way.

What does it mean to be conformed? It is an outward expression that does not come from within. Therefore, it does not represent the Holy Spirit. The way you and I talked, lived, and acted when we were in the world, did not come from the inside of us. It came from the devil and the world outside. What God is saying now is to quit conforming. Don't continue to express, walk, talk, and act like you used to. That's conformity. I will give you an example. We occasionally go down to Honduras. When we are there we conform to many of the laws and rules of Honduras. I went to the Philippine Islands a couple of years ago and did a lot of conforming to their laws also, because it was another country. I am born of God and I am now in another country. I am to conform to the laws and rules of the kingdom of God now. What about the laws and rules of man? I will conform to them only if they do not contradict the laws and rules of God.

Being conformed is being patterned after some definite thing. You and I were patterned after some definite things before we came to Jesus. Those things were of the devil because he is the god of this world. He taught you to kick, fight, be angry, frustrated and fearful. He taught you to hate, to be resentful, bitter, insecure, unloved, unwanted and unworthy. That is what most people conform to. They are still filled with all that they had before they came to Jesus. Their spirits got saved, but everything else is still serving the devil most of the time. They say, "I don't understand why God does not bless me." It is because the mind has not been renewed so that it can line up with their spirit, which is now born of God. Once the mind gets renewed, you can line it up with the spirit.

Conformity is masquerading in the mannerisms, speech, expression, styles and habits of this world which you are no longer to represent. The Word of God says in II Corinthians 5:20, "NOW THEN WE ARE AMBASSADORS FOR CHRIST . . ." We ought to represent our kingdom. You are not to represent the world any longer. You are to represent Almighty God, your Father. However, if you keep on living, walking and talking like you did in the past, you are still representing the other world that you were born into. God wants us to quit masquerading. The world curses, but our language is "Praise God!" That agitates the world more than if you were to say something bad. Saying, "Jesus" burns them. Go to your job and say, "Glory to God! This is the day that the Lord has made." They will say, "There is a place for that." Quit masquerading like the heathen. If they curse in front of you, speak God's language in front of them. We will see whose words are stronger. It is time for God's people to realize who and what they are in Christ Jesus. You have the authority. You are right and they are wrong. If my saying words of praise to God disturbs and frustrates them, it will not cause me to stop. They don't like to hear the Word because it makes them feel filthy inside. The Word of God bothers the devil and his kids. You may say, "But that's my husband, son, momma, etc." If they are not saved, you should get your faith working to get them into God's camp. That's a good reason for you to get your mind renewed and quit masquerading. God does want them saved.

I will give you some examples. Most people, when they get their food in a restaurant, just dive right in. Many of God's people just quietly say, "Thank You, Jesus," instead of boldly asking God to bless their food. You are masquerading and trying to hide your identity. If you say, "Father, in the Name of Jesus, bless this food," everyone stares at you.

My family and I were in a restaurant one day and I made a phone call while waiting for our order. In the conversation I was saying, "Praise God! Glory to Jesus!" I did not think anything of it. When I walked out my two daughters said, "Daddy, you started saying it and the people just looked." The world will curse and think nothing of it. Well, I praise the Lord and think nothing of it, because that is my way of life now.

I am going to use another example about being conformed. This is an example Brother John Osteen used. He and his family were at a football game. Behind them were seated three drunks with their whiskey bottles, to keep themselves warm in the cold weather. They were cursing and cursing, and John just sat there for a few minutes. After a while he just turned around, looked at them, and said, "Praise the Lord! Praise the Lord! Praise the Lord!" The drunks looked at him like he was crazy and they moved to other seats. If he would have sat there and let his ears be filled with that filthy language, that would have been conformity.

You may say, "Well, I don't want to bother the men on the job." What you are doing is conforming, because you know that if you bless your food they are going to call you a holy Joe. They are going to look at you and say, "There is a place in church for that." I would tell them that I am in church, because Jesus is in me. We are talking about conquering the mind for Jesus, and not for the world. No one has to teach you how to get angry, frustrated, confused, discouraged, etc. You have been trained, and when you conform to that, the devil is your master. We were his slaves, but Jesus Christ, the Son of God, is raising up an army of men and women who are going to walk in the fulness of the Holy Spirit of God and be lights to this world. Being light means that you are not like them. This is what God is talking about today. We are no longer to represent the habits of this world. I don't represent the devil or the lost man. I represent Jesus Christ, the Son of God. I am supposed to act like my Father.

God says to "Be not conformed." As long as you do conform to the world, it is because your mind is like their minds. As long as your mind is like theirs, you are going to talk, walk, and think like them. When you get your mind in line with the Word of God you are going to walk, talk, think, and act differently. God is raising you up so that those in the world who don't know Jesus can come to know Him through you.

3. "TO THIS WORLD" In telling us not to be conformed to this world, God is telling us to stop taking on the mannerisms, speech and habit patterns of the people of this world. He wants us to represent His world. The definition of the word "world" is: a floating mass of thoughts. God says, "Don't be conformed to this world's thoughts, opinions, speculations, hopes, impulses, aims and aspirations that are current in the world at any time. What does this world think about insurance? They say to get it. God says not to be conformed to the world's thoughts. What does this world think about credit and medicine? Psalm 1:1 says, "BLESSED IS THE MAN THAT WALKETH NOT IN THE COUNSELF OF THE UNGODLY." That aggravates people. When you start hitting their security it will shake them up. It is impossible to accurately define many of these things concerning the floating mass of thought and opinions. For example, you cannot tell a woman the length she should wear a dress, or how much makeup she should or should not wear. Beware of these thoughts and opinions. Seek the Holy Spirit to find out where to pin them down. He will show you personally.

Saints, find out what the world says, and go the other way. I have my opinions and I live by them, but I cannot accurately define them for you because they are a floating mass of opinion. This is the Greek concept of what this word "world" means. You cannot accurately define it, but it constitutes an effective power of influences. If you don't conform to this world and its demands, people will ridicule you. I will give you an example. Women in pentecostal backgrounds wear long sleeves. All other women outside of that background ridicule and mock them. Why do those ladies bother everyone else? Watch the kids in school, for another example. If the crowd goes to slim pants, they are all going to want to have tight ones too. If the style goes to the big legs, they are all going to want to have big-legged pants. If they don't have what the crowd has, they feel out of place.

The opinions of the world have an influence on your life. This is why Jesus said, "BE NOT CONFORMED TO THIS WORLD." He told us to watch its power and influence. It will demand you to be like it. If you don't, it will call you an odd ball, old-fashioned, and it will laugh at you. I have had many people say, "Brother Willis, you are just old-fashioned about the Bible." I am just as old-fashioned as my Father is. He has never changed? He is eternal. That is how old-fashioned I am. What you will have to begin to do is to break that conformity and really be a light in this dark world.

We are discussing marks of an improper foundation. If you conform to the world you will have a proper foundation to be approved by the world, but you will have an improper foundation to be a good Christian. If you don't conform to the patterns of the world, you have the proper foundation to be accepted and approved by God. In this case the world will mock and ridicule you and withhold their stamp of approval from you. At the same time, God is on the other side of the fence blessing you. It is just a matter of the Christian deciding who he will conform to. You have to either conform to God or the world. If you are conforming to the world, you are not conforming to God. If your life is like everyone else's, you are hidden and no one can spot you. Have you ever seen a drunk in a crowd who went unnoticed? The Bible says, "AND BE NOT DRUNK WITH WINE, WHEREIN IS EXCESS; BUT BE FILLED WITH THE SPIRIT." (Ephesians 5:18) You should be like a drunk in a crowd. They should all know where you are. A drunk in a crowd may be over here, over there, and back over here. You can distinguish him by his talk, his walk, and his action. You can find him. I believe that when a man or woman is serving the Lord Jesus Christ they are going to stand out like a drunk in a crowd. The world says, "Conform. Don't bother me by talking about Jesus. Leave me alone. I'm going to curse like a sailor, and don't say anything about it. Don't mention

Jesus to me." That is what they say. They don't necessarily say it to you directly, but they say it. What they are actually saying is, "Let me do what I want to do and you respect me." Do not respect the devil, Saints. They are protected by the devil. When you respect them when they are wrong, you are respecting the devil. When you do not bow down and conform, they are going to know where you stand. Then if their mother or someone is sick and they need help, they will know where to go, because they have been seeing you even though they have been ridiculing and mocking you. When they have a need they will ease up to you and say, "Would you pray for me?" You will reply, "Yes, I will be glad to." We should not have resentment toward them. We are wise enough to know better because our minds have been renewed. We are wise not to conform to them in the way we talk, walk and act. We are wise enough to act like God so that when they do have troubles and want to find God, we can help them. How would they ever find Jesus through you if you conform to them? The disapproval of the world comes automatically, but God's approval is upon you, as a Christian.

The Bible is like a paradox. Jesus says, "BLESSED ARE YE, WHEN MEN SHALL REVILE YOU, AND PERSECUTE YOU, AND SHALL SAY ALL MANNER OF EVIL AGAINST YOU FALSELY, FOR MY· SAKE" (Matthew 5:11). The world says that if you are reviled and persecuted, you are in bad shape and you are not blessed. Jesus says you are blessed.

I will never forget when God spoke that Scripture to me. I was in the First Baptist Church in Baldwin, Louisiana, about eight years ago. I had received the baptism of the Holy Spirit with the evidence of speaking in tongues. I was casting out devils, and preaching it all in the Baptist church. As a result, I was reviled and persecuted. From that time on, everywhere I went I ran into preachers with whom I had attended college and seminary. They all reviled and persecuted me until it was getting very hard on me. Everyone was rejecting me and saying I was crazy, but the Word said it would be that way. One day Jesus spoke to me and said, "Son, blessed are you when you are reviled and persecuted for My Name's sake." At that point I started going out shouting a little more. I said, "Lord, let them give me some more, because I want to be blessed more. Let them laugh at me some more, Lord. I will take more blessing, because I am going to magnify and glorify Jesus. I'm going to speak it from the roof top." Everywhere I go I am going to shout that "Jesus is Lord, Saviour, Baptizer, Healer, Deliverer, Protector and Provider! Jesus is coming!" If they want to ridicule that, they have problems. However, someone must broadcast it. Someone has to be bold enough with the Holy Spirit to let them know that God is God of this world and that Jesus is Lord. The lives of the bold ones will let them know that there is a better way.

III. CONFUSION is another mark of an improper foundation. II Thessalonians 2:2 says, "THAT YE BE NOT SOON SHAKEN IN MIND, OR BE TROUBLED, NEITHER BY SPIRIT, NOR BY WORD, NOR BY LETTER AS FROM US . . . " Paul said not to be shaken by spirit. If those pressures begin to come to you, don't be shaken about them. Don't be shaken by words that come against you. God has warned us against being shaken by mental agitation, disturbance of poise, becoming off-balanced or swayed by our senses. If the enemy can come against you by bringing agitation, annoyance, disturbance of poise, getting you off-balanced or swayed by your senses, you have let him get to your mind. When a mind is programmed and renewed by the Word of God, the devil cannot do that to you. Someone could slap you, and you would say, "Glory to God!" They could get up and walk out, and you would just say, "Hallelujah! Thank You, Jesus," because your mind has been renewed by the Word. The Word of God says in Philippians 4:4 to "REJOICE IN THE LORD ALWAYS: AND AGAIN I SAY, REJOICE." Any time you are shaken or troubled in mind, an outside force has caused a rocking motion. You can liken the rocking to a building shaken by an earthquake or a ship that has been blown away because it has been insecurely anchored during a storm. What Paul is saying is for us not to be troubled or shaken in mind. Don't let any outside force, whether it be the devil, people, words, circumstances or situations, begin to cause you to rock and lose your poise.

I will give you an example. You are all fired up hearing the Word of God and you determine that you are going to go out to your job and really be a witness for Jesus. You get out on the job and one of the men says something to you. You reply, "Jesus loves you!" He slaps you on the face with the look of hatred on his face. What do you say? The next day you go to work but you decide that it would be wisdom to sneak up on him to lead him to Jesus. Therefore, you spend the next two years trying to sneak up on him. It is the outside forces that caused you to rock and back down from speaking the good news. You have let the devil in the man be stronger than Jesus in you.

Paul said not to be shaken, but be controlled by a mind enlightened by revelation of God's Word. If someone curses you, just smile and say, "Jesus loves you and I do, too!" Speak the Word and let Jesus work for you. God wants your mind to be controlled by a revelation of His Word. You will never be able to walk in the fulness of the things of God until you bring your mind under submission to the Holy Spirit of God. It's your mind; you have the right to control it; you have the right for your mind to think good things, the things of God. God inside of you desires to control your mind, but Satan outside desires to control your mind. And your mind is as much yours as your hand. That mind of yours, Saints, under the leadership of the Holy Spirit of God, can be disciplined to hold fast to the beautiful truth of God's Word. You can reject the fear, you can reject the hurt and the resentment, and the disappointments, the insecurities and all the things that come to your mind, which is the real battlefield for you to grow to maturity in Christ. Salvation comes instantly, but the renewal of the mind is progressive; it is a day to day battle, to reconquer that which is yours. The mind is yours, Saints, but while you were heathen, while you were lost, while you knew not Jesus Christ the Son of God, Satan came in and took control of your mind. He trained your mind; he programmed your mind just as a man does a computer today. But now God is coming with His Word and we are beginning to come into our inheritance, and that is a mind that can continue to meditate and concentrate upon the things of God; a mind that knows the Word of God, so when the Spirit of God speaks to you, He can communicate to your mind, and you obey the things of God.

Revelation is the transfer of knowledge from the spirit to the soul, to the mind, so you can act upon it in this world, that Jesus Christ might be glorified. If Satan is continually controlling your mind with fears, and frustrations, and disappointments, and hurts and insecurities and inferiorities, then you will never be able to hear from the Holy Spirit of God. Your life will be up and down, off and on, and hot and cold. Sometimes you'll be on fire for God, and sometimes He will seem like He's so far off you don't know what to do. Sometimes the joy just bursts forth out of you and sometimes you can hardly make yourself smile, because the enemy has control of your mind.

What I'm doing is showing you some things that could be the reason you are unable to control your mind. Then we will go to the proper foundation, and you will be able to lay the right kind of foundation. Wrong motives produce wrong action that exposes the roots. It says in Matthew 6:33, "SEEK YE FIRST THE KINGDOM OF GOD AND HIS RIGHTEOUS-NESS," and if you're not careful you will not be seeking first the kingdom, you will be seeking the things. You will be seeking a husband, a wife, a new car, a new home, a promotion in your business. None of these things are wrong in themselves, but Jesus said if you seek Him first He will give all these things to you. He says He will promote you; He says everything you put your hands on will prosper. God will prosper you if the motives are right. He will provide you a husband, He will provide you a wife, He will provide the automobiles and the homes and those things, but you must make sure that your motives are right.

Whenever confusion hits your mind, rebuke the devil. God is the author of peace for Christians. Confusion is for the lost people; that's normal, that's all they know; they can't have the God kind of peace. They are trying to get it, but they can't get it. All they can have is what the world offers. Because you are the children of God, you can have what God offers you. He offers you peace. He says, "My peace I give unto you, not as the world gives." He says, "My love I give unto you, not as the world gives." So, Saints, if it is not as the world gives, you have to find it in a different way. It will produce a different effect in your life. Any time confusion comes, remember, God is not the author of it. If the enemy is able to get to your mind and get you frustrated, confused, and upset and agitated, Satan became the god of your mind. Confusion became the god of your mind, and confusion is of the devil. Rebel against confusion, because it is a sign of an improper foundation. Rebel against conformity to the world, because it is a sign of an improper foundation.

IV.   FALLING is another mark of an improper foundation. Hebrews 12:3 "Be wearied and faint in your minds."

1. "FAINT IN YOUR MINDS" The words, "faint in your minds," is a reverse of vigor and cheerfulness. When faith is not operative we are left to cope with the situation with the power of the natural mind, which cannot stand the pressure of the enemy. You are saved, it happens instantly; you receive Jesus Christ as your personal Saviour. But the mind is not instantly renewed; you must begin to study the Word of God. Line upon line, precept upon precept, concept upon concept. Your minds are renewed like you learn engineering, or carpentry, or painting, or plumbing, or law, or anything else; you begin line upon line, precept upon precept. What happens when you get saved is that the devil begins to come against your mind, because he knows that you are saved. He even knows that you are filled with the Holy Spirit. He knows that the Holy Spirit inside of you will never be able to do much through you if he can keep your mind confused. He therefore attempts to keep you conforming to the world with the wrong motives and keep enough pressure on you so you grow weary and faint in your mind. When faith is not operative we are left to cope with situations with the power of the natural mind. This is why you must learn faith. If you don't know how to move in faith, when pressure comes, when trouble comes, when problems come, you are going to try to cope with them with the natural mind, and you can't do it. You will blow it every time. That's

why your faith is going to be operative and you are learning to trust God, because if you don't the pressure is going to cause you to be weary and you will faint in your mind.

2. "WEARIED" This word, "wearied," means you get exhausted. You will get despondent. For example: you believe in God for healing and the devil keeps putting pressure on your mind. What happens? He puts pain in your body, and it gets worse and worse; next thing you know, you get exhausted, despondent. Here you are, a loyal servant of the Lord Jesus Christ; the devil does not want you to conquer your mind; he doesn't want you to bring it under control. So what is he doing? Through circumstances and situations, and people bombarding you and jumping on you, he's trying to cause you to be exhausted and despondent. He will keep the difficulties coming. All your mind is thinking on is this trouble, this problem, thinking on this, thinking on that. After a while you don't have enough time for the Word, you don't have much time to speak in tongues, you don't have the desire to really praise God. You're getting weary. The fire that was once there begins to go down; the fire gets lower and lower, and lower and lower, and next thing you faint in your mind. You try to hold to your confession, but after a while you faint in your mind. You give him four, five, six months, and the devil is trying to tear down everything you have. He says, "Prosperity doesn't work; it just works for Reverend Willis, but it is not going to work for you. It works for Joe there, but it's not going to work for you," and the next thing you know the pressure gets you and you faint in your mind. Saints, whenever you are falling like that, it is a sign that you need to conquer your mind. If these kinds of things are happening, then your mind is not under the control of the Holy Spirit. If you get weary and faint in your mind because of pressure, if you give up, you blow. Sometimes you hold in there for two or three months, six months; but the next thing you know, you can't take it any more and you fall. If you've been doing that, it's another sign or mark of an improper foundation. I don't like to show the negative points, but I need to show them so that you can find yourself, and we can help you locate yourself -- then we can start doing some surgery,

and get your mind conquered by the Word of God.

What is the result of a person who gets weary and faints in his mind? Partial or complete abandonment of his vows and the stand he once made for God. Example: you are believing God for your husband to be saved. He comes home at night and slaps you across the face. Well, you do pretty good, but the next night he doesn't come home at all. And after two or three months like that you get weary, tired of fighting, agitated, aggravated, and you faint in your mind. Whenever you do that, what happens is that you partially or completely abandon your vows and your stand for Jesus Christ. Why? Because you failed and you let the devil take control of your mind. You let him put the pressure on your mind until you couldn't hold to the Word. That is a sign that your mind is not renewed. When you can't hold to the Word continually and consistently, your mind is not renewed by that Word yet; this is why there is a struggle, this is why the failures come. Until you get your mind renewed with the Word of God, you will be up and down, off and on, and hot and cold. You will be just as saved as I am, just as filled with the Holy Spirit as I am, even operating in the gifts, but your life won't be on a level plateau.

V.   TALKATIVENESS. This is another mark of an improper foundation. A mouth that cannot be controlled is a sign of an improper foundation. A running tongue -- Proverbs 29:11 says, "A FOOL UTTERETH ALL HIS MIND , , ," "Well, I'm going to speak my mind" -- that's a sign of a fool. When they are speaking their mind, watch them. " . . .BUT A WISE MAN KEEPETH IT IN TILL AFTERWARDS." A wise man can keep his tongue under control when the situations and circumstances come.

1.   Untrained minds will speak forth bad confessions, gossip, foolish things and irrelevant things. If your mind is untrained, it's going to come out of your mouth. Conception takes place in the womb and the birth is on the way. That birth has to be aborted, or either the birth will come forth. The same is true with a thought. A thought comes to your mind, is conceived; you become pregnant in the mind with a thought. You become

24

pregnant with an evil thought. Now, when a woman is pregnant, there must be an abortion or a birth. When your mind is impregnated with an evil thought, you either have to abort it or give birth. When the pregnancy comes about, birth doesn't happen right then; usually it takes nine months. There is a period of time between conception and birth. When something gets birthed out of your mouth, you did not conceive it right then. It was already planted, it was born, you've been watering it, you've been feeding it. The thought is born in your mind, and you feed it and it gets a little bigger, and a little bigger, and after a while it gets so big you can't hold it in your mind any more, and that's why you let it out. Unrenewed minds will speak forth bad confessions. If under pressure you speak forth bad confessions, it is a mark that your mind is not renewed. Let me give you an example. Put four people together. While one of them is talking the other three are thinking what they are going to say; they are not listening to you. You want me to show you how you can prove it? You put four people together: one will tell something here, next thing you know another one will say something totally unrelated to what the others have said. When you get through, you have four people who are talking about four different things. But each one of them is trying to show you how it ties with the first thing. You cut out a great deal of your talking, when you realize this principle.

  2. **It can be hidden, but often pressure reveals it.** The thoughts in your mind that are birthed there will come forth. A lot of times you are strong enough to hide them for a season, but after a while the pressure bursts it forth. Have you ever had something in your mind for two or three months, but all at once some pressure comes before you and you spit it out? First thing you say is, "Oh, I'm sorry." You fed that thought so long it had to be born. You need to confess that sin, and ask the one you hurt to forgive you. "But if they hadn't done it to me, I wouldn't have said it!" You said it; you control your own mouth; it's yours. Your hand doesn't run wild, does it? It just doesn't reach out and hit someone, and then you say, "I'm sorry; I didn't mean to hit you upside the head." You would say, "You are lying; you did it on purpose." When people shoot

that stuff out of their mouths they do it on purpose, and then they are going to try to cover it up. When they get through they feel so bad about it, but you know what they're feeling bad about? They got caught! They are not really sorry for you. They are sorry because they revealed themselves, they brought forth their colors. "Brother Willis, how do you know so much about this?" I've been there; I've opened my mouth before. But immediately I said, "Forgive me, Lord Jesus, forgive me." When you open the faucet all the way, you can't just cut it off with one touch. Usually you won't shut it off until you let all the garbage out. We are talking about marks of an improper foundation to conquer your mind. The key to really walking with the Lord is being honest with yourselves. You are the biggest deceiver in the world. The biggest liar in the world is somebody who lies to himself. Any time you contradict the Word of God, you are wrong. I don't care what you think, or your opinion -- you are wrong; God is right.

VI.   INSTABILITY, James 1:8 "A DOUBLEMINDED MAN IS UNSTABLE IN ALL HIS WAYS." This word, "double-minded," means a two-souled man, a two-faced man. The word "doubleminded" means unsteady; he's fickle, he wobbles, he reels as a drunk man or as cork on water. If you are unable to conquer your mind, this is probably one of your marks - you are unsteady. Sometimes you praise God, and sometimes you say, "Well, I don't know if these tongues are real." Individuals like that are unstable, and the Bible says they are unstable in ALL their ways. Until you get to the place where you can continually praise God, all the time, regardless of the problem, you are doubleminded, you are two-faced. If you can't rejoice in the Lord always, the Bible says you are two-faced, you are doubleminded. One time you have hunger for the Word of God, the fire is burning inside you; and next time you can go for weeks and not even open it up. One time your face is toward the Word; next time your face is away from it. Two-faced. You cannot choose decisively, you can't really choose to stay with God, because there is instability about you in all your ways.

26

Whenever a person is unstable, here are two things that happen:

1. **He disqualifies himself from much of God's blessing,** because James 1:7 says, "LET NOT THAT MAN THINK HE SHALL RECEIVE ANYTHING OF THE LORD." You disqualify yourself when you are two-faced. You must come to the place that your mind is under control.

You are saved, filled with the Holy Ghost, and you love God. This study guide is not about your love toward God. It has nothing to do with that; this has to do with the conquest of your mind, so God can use you mightily through Jesus Christ. Today, God is raising up an army of men and women who are going to be used mightily by Him. How can you be used mightily by God? Have a mind that is conquered, so that the Holy Spirit can speak to you with regularity, because your mind is always thinking on God. But when that mind is not "stayed on Him," God inside of you can't speak to you and therefore can't guide you. All believers desire to be guided, but a requirement for guidance is to have your mind conquered by the Word of God.

2. **A person who is unstable disqualifies himself, and he** therefore does not receive. Then he moves into hypocrisy and abandonment of the things of God. God says, in I John 4:4, "GREATER IS HE THAT IS IN YOU THAN HE THAT IS IN THE WORLD." He said, "I put My Spirit in you so that you can reign, so you can rule in all things." You are qaualified as you conquer your mind. I'm teaching you all this so you can good servant of the Lord Jesus, but you must be teachable. I believe you are, by faith, if not by fact.

VII. **MISDIRECTION.** Ephesians 4:17 says, "WALK NOT AS OTHER GENTILES WALK. . ." And what are Gentiles in the Bible? Lost people, those who do not know Jesus Christ as Saviour. They walk " . . . IN THE VANITY OF THEIR MIND." Let's see what he means by the vanity of their mind.

1. **"WALK NOT"** He says do not conduct or order your behavior in the direction of the heathen. Who is a heathen?

A man who doesn't confess Jesus Christ as his Lord and Saviour. When you observe the life and actions of those who do not profess Jesus Christ as their Lord and Saviour and you see how they talk, then you say, "I can't talk like that any more." They have their language, you have yours: "Glory, Hallelujah, Praise God, Thank You Jesus, I bless your Holy Name." Some will say, "I don't want to hear that stuff." Well, "You worship your god, I'll worship mine. You magnify yours, I have a right to magnify mine." The ungodly do not look at it that way. If you say something about their cursing, they say you're getting on them, but if they say something to you about praising Jesus, it's all right? The world says, "Leave me alone, don't bother me." You don't have to say anything; just mind your own business, praise the Lord, and it will shake everything everywhere you go.

In Matthew 6:33 Jesus says "these things shall be added unto you." Let me explain. The lost people of the world are out there with their dreams, their aspirations, their ambitions, their goals and they are striving, they are working, they are plotting, they are planning; but what does God tell you to do? He says, "WALK NOT AS OTHER BENTILES WALK, IN THE VANITY OF THEIR MIND." Don't conduct yourself like them. "What am I going to do?" Let all your goals, your dreams, your aspirations and all your planning be to learn about Jesus Christ, the Son of God, and learn the Word of God and the things of God; and God says, if you do that, "I will add unto you all the things they seek after." The only way they can get ahead out there is to strive, to strain, plot, plan and drive with ambition, and the Bible calls it the vanity of the mind. They get the things, but the things do not satisfy them. "You be faithful to Me and, " God says, "I will give you every thing they are seeking after." Jesus says, "SEEK YE FIRST THE KINGDOM OF GOD, AND HIS RIGHTEOUSNESS ; AND ALL THESE THINGS SHALL BE ADDED UNTO YOU." The world says you can't get it that way, you have to give a little time to God, and a little time to the things of God; now you have to have balance in this thing, you have to be reasonable. God says, "You put Me first, and I will make you so good out there until it just catches up with you." He says, "I will

28

make you a good painter, plumber, carpenter, or whatever you are. I will give you favor; I will bless you."

2. "VANITY OF MIND" What does Ephesians 4:17 mean by vanity of their mind? That which is aimless, resultless, futile except in mind of the ungodly; is void of real worth. He says, "Don't walk according to the vanity of the mind." That means all those things that the world seeks after are futile. You can save and save to get a new car, and when you get it you are excited. You keep it clean, you wash it, you keep the carpets clean for about two or three weeks; but soon the excitement fades. The things of the world are beckoning fantasies which appear to be real and satisfying. It's fantasy. You fantasize how nice it would be to be driving that new car, how it would be to be living in that home; you fantasize how that vacation will be. You fantasize about that home, and plan and strive for ten or fifteen years. The next thing you know you get it, and the thrill is over. Do you know why? It's just wood and brick, and it's going to continue to depreciate. You are going to have to repaint it and clean it. It will rot, it will tear up, it can be blown away; and here you are, putting all your life into getting such garbage as that. You know what God says: "Seek Me first; all these things I will give to you, because I don't need them."

The beckoning of fantasy, which appears to be real and satisfying, of real value, but upon reception has no satisfying influence! If wealth, and cars, and homes, and social security, and bank accounts would satisfy, the world would be floating with happy people. They all have a bank account; they may just have fifty dollars in savings, but boy, that's important to them. I'll never forget when I was in Baldwin, Louisiana. I put $200 in my savings account and never did add to it for five years. I was praying one day and God told me to go to Mobile, Alabama. I was asking God and believing Him to give me the money to go, and God spoke to me and said, "Son, don't you dare ask me for something I have already given you." I said, "God, what do you mean? All I have is about $10 in the bank." He said, "What about that savings account?" I said, "But God, I'm saving that for a rainy day." He said, "Yes, I know." You know what I was saving it for? A rainy day, and it's going to rain. I took that $200 and went to Mobile and had a good time. It appears to be of value, but be willing to turn it loose. Many believe a nice car will satisfy, but it won't do it. Many believe a nice home will satisfy, but it won't do it. Some believe success will satisfy. When you get one success, what do you want? Another one. You want the feeling for another one, and the devil gives you a good feeling for that success; then you want to get another success to get that feeling again. So the devil has you working all your life for a feeling. But you that are born of God can know the truth and seek first the kingdom of God, aim at the things of God, strive toward the things of God. Let Christ reign and rule in your life, and as Christ reigns and rules in your life he will bring you into a new land of victory. In your talk and your walk as sons of God, children of the King, you will know real peace, and people will think you're crazy because you have peace. They say you can't live that way. You will know real joy. I go all around the country and God gives me His joy, and you know people think I'm crazy because I enjoy myself so much? I have what they want, and they think I'm crazy! But I want you to know I didn't get it from man, it comes from God -- Praise God! You can't get it from man, you can't get it from the world, you must get it from God. He is the only Giver of the things that last. "Oh foolish Christians, who has bewitched you, who has deceived you that you should not obey the truth of the Word?" He says, seek ye first the kingdom of God.

Jesus desires His followers to be a light out there, because they are searching for reality, but the only way they are going to find it is in Jesus. The only way they are going to find Jesus is that you are out there shining. This bright light of mine, I'm going to let it shine! But the world says, "I'm going to put your light out; I'm going to make you shut up; I'm going to make you stop praising God. I'm going to make you stop saying 'Jesus,' I'm going to wipe that smile off your face, I'll make you be like me: mad, angry, fearful, frustrated, confused." That's what the world says. I keep on saying, "This bright light of mine, I'm going to let it shine," and the only way I can let my light shine is to conquer my mind with the Word of God.

Matthew 6:33 says, "SEEK YE FIRST THE KINGDOM OF GOD." In His Word God promises you love, joy, peace, health, prosperity, faith, anointing, answered prayers, etc. However, it is not until your mind is renewed by the Word that you will be able to receive these promises. If your mind is not secure in the Word, you let the devil control it and he robs you of the promises.

OUTLINE ... CHAPTER TWO
Marks of a Proper Foundation

INTRODUCTION

Conquest of the mind is progressive, and the key to receiving revelation from Holy Spirit, to be translated into action to glorify God.

I.   AN HONEST MIND: I Chron. 28:9 "Serve him with a perfect heart (II Cor. 5:17) and with a willing mind: for the Lord searcheth the hearts and understandeth all the imaginations of the thoughts."

    1.   An honest mind knows scriptural disobedience can be with the mind.
    2.   Failure not revealed by outward evidence signifies an inward problem.

II. A TEACHABLE MIND: Acts 17:11-12 "These were more noble than those in Thessalonica, in that they received the word with all readiness of mind and searched the scriptures daily whether those things were so." Therefore, many of them believed because they were teachable.

    1.   Noble: True spirited - positive, not negative with word.
    2.   Readiness of mind: Came to believe - eager - open.
    3.   "Believed:" Result - verdict - spontaneous outcome.

Rom. 8:6 "To be carnally minded (hostile to Word, flesh and world controlled) is death, but to be spiritually minded is life and peace." What you receive locates you.

III.   A TRANSFORMED MIND: Rom. 12:2 "But be ye transformed by the renewing of your mind."

1.   A two-fold process of renovation and rewiring.
2.   Steady advancing to follow God's spiritual truths.
3.   Continual ordering of behavior within sphere of Word.
4.   A new mentality that no longer judges or understands as it once did. Now it is keyed to finding and following God.
5.   Gives knowledge to avoid conformity to this world.
6.   Conduct reflects pilgrims, not citizens of this world.
7.   Knows howling with wolves is costly.

IV.   A POWERFUL MIND: II Cor. 10:5 "Casting down imaginations and every high thing that exalteth itself against the knowledge of God and bringing into captivity every thought to the obedience of Christ."

1.   Casting down: wrecking - demolishing - put to sword-cut off.
2.   Imaginations: reasoning - argument - question as all are hostile devices, schemes and concoction to Word.
3.   Thought: product of intelligent mind - result of thinking. Against the knowledge (Word) of God.

V.   A DISCIPLINED MIND: Neh. 4:6 "the people had a mind to work" Study is work - strenuous - requires energy, so most do very little.

II Tim. 2:15 - Jos. 1:8 - Psalm 1:2 - I Pet. 1:13 - Phil. 4:7 - Isa. 26:3.

CHAPTER TWO
Marks of a Proper Foundation

INTRODUCTION: Conquest of the mind is progressive and the key to receiving revelation from the Holy Spirit, to be translated into action on your part to glorify God. Your mind being renewed is the key. You have been saved, baptized in the Holy Spirit, you need to know divine healing, speak in tongues, move in the gifts. But if your mind is not renewed you will never come to the place where you can really move with God. The conquest of the. mind is progressive, you don't get this over night. You have to stay with it week after week, year after year, and realize it is the key to receiving revelation from the Holy Spirit.

The word "revelation" means transfer of knowledge from the spirit to the soul. The Holy Spirit is in you now, you are the temple of the Holy Spirit, so the Spirit of God (John 16:13 calls Him the Spirit of Truth), the Spirit of Truth, lives in me. When you begin to understand this you will not be looking to God for some mystical understanding or revelation about God.

You begin to understand that the Spirit of Truth lives right in you. He has the mind of God. All the knowledge of God is in your spirit, but unless it is transferred to your mind (so you know how to put it in action), it will never be of any value to you. Many Christians today are saved and filled with the Holy Spirit but their lives never glorify God, and they have just as much of the Spirit of Truth and all the knowledge that you and I have; be just as saved as we are, speak in tongues just like we do, go to the same heaven, but their lives down here will be incomplete. They will never reach the fulfillment of the great

things that God has in store for them down here, because He desires this revelation to be translated into action here in this world, that God might be glorified. As you learn how to walk and talk as sons and daughters of the King then it is translated into action, and other people see that action and come to know Jesus, that Jesus might be glorified. It makes your life change, makes your life count. In the Baptist churches we talked about stars in your crown. There are Scriptures that indicate stars in your crown, and stars in your crown can easily be those whom you win to the Lord Jesus Christ. How many stars are there going to be in your crown? Is your light shining? Don't let the devil put it out.

I.   AN HONEST MIND: You must be honest with yourself. Dishonesty is bad enough, but when someone is dishonest with himself, it is deceiving. I Chronicles 28:9 says "SERVE HIM WITH A PERFECT HEART." II Corinthians 5:17 shows that you and I can serve Him with a perfect heart. "THEREFORE IF ANY MAN BE IN CHRIST, HE IS A NEW CREATURE: OLD THINGS ARE PASSED AWAY; BEHOLD, ALL THINGS ARE BECOME NEW." We have that perfect heart of God now. The Old Testament speaks about the circumcision of flesh, but

God says if you and I have the circumcision of the heart, we can serve the Lord with a perfect heart and with a willing mind. A lot of people are serving God but not really with a willing mind. They come in with their heels dug in. They feel that they are forced to study, forced into praising God. So, therefore, they have an unwilling mind to do the things of God. You want to do your own thing. You don't want anything that you feel has been imposed upon you. You feel that maybe God is taking advantage of you, when He actually is requiring it of you. He says serve Him with a "PERFECT HEART AND WITH A WILLING MIND: FOR THE LORD SEARCHETH ALL HEARTS AND UNDERSTANDETH ALL THE IMAGINATIONS OF THE THOUGHTS." It is an amazing thing that Christians somehow or other think they can think what they want to think. "Yes, I can think what I want to think." No, you can't, not as a Christian who desires to obey the Word. You can't drive like you want to drive and obey the law. As a Christian you don't have a right to think like you want to think anymore. You don't have a right to think evil anymore; you gave it up when you came to Jesus. You don't have the right to think hate; you don't have the right to think envy or bitterness or jealousy, or evil things about anybody anytime. You don't have that right anymore, because you know what the Bible says? "HE SEARCHETH THE HEARTS AND UNDERSTANDETH ALL THE IMAGINATIONS OF THE THOUGHTS."

1. Scriptural Disobedience Can Be with the Mind. Philippians 4:8 says, only think on those things that are just, holy, pure, lovely, honest, of good report, of virtue, and praise. If we don't obey that we are coming to Scriptural disobedience with the mind. Many people think that disobedience is just what you do outside. The inward man can disobey God, too. Only think on those things that are just, holy, pure, lovely, honest, of good report, virtuous and praiseworthy. My hand doesn't run wild and go where it wants to go; it goes where I tell it to go. My feet don't run wild and take off by themselves; I control them. Through the Holy Spirit of God that dwells in you, you can bring your mind under the control and submission

to the Holy Spirit, to think only in line with the Holy Spirit. Imagine your mind thinking on good things, pure, wholesome, healthy things, what it will begin to do in your life. It will grow a crop of goodness. But, you see, as long as the Devil can keep your mind thinking on other things, you grow the wrong crop. A crop of meanness, envy, anger, bitterness, and jealousy, frustration, confusion, fear, disappointment; because, Saints, you need to realize that your mind is the battlefield. The Holy Spirit from the inside desires to control it, and the devil from without.

2. **Failure Not Revealed by the Outward Evidence Signifies an Inward Problem.** The failure is not revealed by any particular outward evidence. I don't see them or you don't see them doing anything that particularly will cause failure. But yet, they can't make it. They are continually not receiving answers to prayer, being defeated here and defeated there, not being able to grasp the things of God. Whenever people are that way, I can tell you, they don't have an honest mind and it proves they have an inward problem.

God is not wrong. God doesn't make the mistakes. So many Christians learn how they ought to act and how they ought to talk, so they do the acting and they do the talking and the walking, but inside they are acting, and in reality they are talking and walking another way. Then they say with their mouth, "I don't understand why I don't receive my answers," when their mind just got through thinking about slapping somebody upside the head. That mind with jealousy and envy, that mind is remembering some stinking old sin that your husband or wife did to you twenty years ago, and you say, "I don't understand why God doesn't answer my prayers; I'm diligent." What with? Not the most important thing! Your mind must be conquered now. I'm not saying this to be hard, I'm saying it to help reveal the truth to you, so you can have an honest mind and really face it. You say, "Wait a minute now. If this thing is not working for me it is not God's fault. I'm just going to have to stay with it until God straightens some things out." Be honest with God: "Father, I don't know where I'm missing

38

you, but Lord God, evidently I'm missing You somewhere; forgive me, Father, wherever I'm missing You. And, Father, I ask You in Jesus' Name, that the Holy Spirit within will show me where I'm missing it. I want to know, God, because I don't want to miss You." I've done this many times. I determined to have an honest mind and a willing mind before God. I just say, "Lord, I know it is not You, so somewhere in this thing, Lord, I have a problem. God, I think it might be this and this, but I don't know. Lord, is something there that I can't recognize because I can't see myself?" (It takes the Holy Spirit to really show it to me.) When I look at me I'm not bad, I'm pretty good. I'm probably the only one who sees myself that way. It takes the Holy Spirit to reveal it to me. So I just say, "Lord, I know since it's been missed it is failure on this end of the line, never Your end of the line. So Father, I ask You in the Name of Jesus that the Spirit of God in me will show me. I receive in Jesus' Name whatever I need to do." Now, get ready. You will be amazed sometimes what He'll show you, and you will think that was John's or Mary's problem. Always realize that Scriptural disobedience can be with your mind. Phil. 4:8 is your key Scripture.

Let's say you are believing God for a healing and you're quoting the Scriptures and you're acting every way you know, yet you can't get a firm hold of the healing. Or you are believing God for some money, and you can't be comfortable that you have received it. Many times the reason you are short-circuiting your faith is because your mind up there is doing some thinking contrary to the Word of God. Have an honest mind.

II.   A TEACHABLE MIND: This is one of the things that I confess all the time. This is one of the keys to maturing in the Lord Jesus Christ. Acts 17: 11-12, "THESE WERE MORE NOBLE THAN THOSE IN THESSALONICA, IN THAT THEY RECEIVED THE WORD WITH ALL READINESS OF MIND, AND SEARCHED THE SCRIPTURES DAILY, WHETHER THOSE THINGS WERE SO. THEREFORE MANY OF THEM BELIEVED." Just being teachable. The Lord spoke to me and told me. "Son, there are three keys to a continuous faith walk." He said, **meekness**, means being teachable toward God. He said, **humility**, means the proper estimation of yourself, not according to the world, but according to the Word. What the Word says about me. It says, "I am more than a conqueror." That's the proper estimation. The Word says, "I can do all things through Jesus Christ who strengthens me." That's a humble estimation of me, because you know who said that? God. The third thing is **gentleness**. Meekness toward God, humility toward self, and gentleness in your outreach to others. If it touched God, it works for you and it touches others. You must have a teachable mind.

1. **A Teachable Mind is Noble.** The word "noble" means true spirited — positive, not negative with the Word. Most people are negative with the Word. They search the Word not to look for the truth of it, to disprove it. You know why ministers sometimes have to minister so strong? Because they have unnoble spirits. They are not positive, they say, "You have to prove it to me before I will believe it." Don't come that way. Come and say, "Praise God, I'm going to look for that Scripture to prove it is right, not to prove it is wrong." Be true spirited, positive, not negative with the Word. What you need to do as you hear preaching, teaching and exhortation is say, "I heard it, I received it, I'm going to lay it beside the Word. If it lines up with the Word I'm going to receive it; if it doesn't line up with the Word, I'm going to lay it aside." Approach it positively, and you will become a lot more teachable. This is one reason why God has blessed me so much. This is one reaosn I know as much as I know about the Bible, because I'm teachable. I'm teachable and I confess every day that I'm a meek man. When God says stop, I stop. He says go, I go. He says give, I give; He says run, I run; He says shout, I shout; He says dance, I dance. I don't question God. I am teachable. You know what I've found out? Usually when I finish with what He tells me to do, He tells me why. But you know why a lot of people don't receive revelations? They say, "God, You tell me why and then I'll do it." You know what you usually get? Nothing! Others become teachable and get all the goodies.

"THESE WERE MORE NOBLE THAN THOSE IN THESSALONICA IN THAT THEY RECEIVED THE WORD WITH ALL READINESS OF MIND." And the readiness of mind means that they came to believe, they came eager, they came open. The Lord showed me some principles early in my Spirit filled life. We had what we called dinner on the grounds, and we had all that food on the tables. I would look at the food and take all I wanted. As I looked at it I would say, "That's good, I'll take some." Some I would look at and immediately I'd say, "that's no good, I don't want that." But some I really didn't know whether it was good or bad, so I would sample it. I'd swallow it, but I still couldn't really tell. Three or four hours later my stomach would start bothering me. My body is made to get rid of the food that ought not be there. The same principle works spiritually. I trust the Holy Spirit in me; He'll be able to get rid of junk that ought not stay in there. But do you realize what a lot of people do? They suffer five, six, seven, eight hours, not being willing to get rid of it.

2. Readiness of Mind. You must have a readiness of mind. When a man or woman comes before God teachable, then automatically they have a noble, true spirit and they have readiness of mind. You know what they're going to receive; they are going to get blessed, they are going to believe and therefore receive. They were "MORE NOBLE THAN THOSE IN THESSALONICA." Are you more noble than those? If you're not, get that way! What does it mean to be more noble? They received the Word with more readiness of mind and they searched the Scriptures daily. Remember -- they didn't search to disprove, they searched to see if it was so. You know I tell people that if they give, God will bless them, and you know what? They keep searching for Scriptures to prove that they don't have to. They ought to try to search the Scriptures so they can get blessed. You tell people that Jesus heals them; you know what they do? They start quoting you Scriptures to prove that He won't. And you're trying to give them something good. Unteachable.

Confess that you won't receive anything that doesn't

line up with the Word of God. You won't have so many difficulties that way.

3. "Believed." Romans 8:6 says, "TO BE CARNALLY MINDED." Carnally minded means hostile to the Word, you are flesh and world controlled. A person who is not teachable is carnally minded; that means they're hostile to the Word, they resist the Word, they keep on saying, "Prove it to me." Just simply believe that God said what He meant, and meant what He said. If I'm drinking any deadly thing in my mind, it is not going to harm me because Jesus is going to make it right. He will help me get rid of it. To be carnally minded is to be hostile to the Word, "BUT TO BE SPIRITUALLY MINDED IS LIFE AND PEACE." What you receive locates you. Question to disprove, not approve. So many people prove they are carnally minded because of their questions, and all their searching to disprove something. The first time you hear something that doesn't line up with what you think, you start searching to disprove it. Don't search to disprove it, search to prove it. A person who is not teachable holds to PRIDE. God wants you to check out the word you hear. So you must have a teachable mind.

III. A TRANSFORMED MIND: This is a sign of a proper foundation. Romans 12:2 says, "AND BE NOT CONFORMED TO THIS WORLD: BUT BE YE TRANSFORMED BY THE RENEWING OF YOUR MIND, THAT YE MAY PROVE WHAT IS THAT GOOD, AND ACCEPTABLE, AND PERFECT WILL OF GOD." God says, don't be conformed; He says, don't be like the world. You can't get it clearer than that. You start telling people some of the things the Bible says, and they get mad at you. And it is just that simple, the Word of God says: don't be like the world. Don't talk like them, don't act like them, and really you're not to dress like them. So God says, be ye transformed by the renewing of your mind.

1. A Two-fold Process of Renovation and Rewiring. Everything that has been put in your mind must be renovated.

42

When you renovate and rewire a house, how do you do it? You strip all the old wires out. They put wires there some fifty or sixty years ago; they're not as good as the wires made today. That old knowledge put there by the world is not as good as this new knowledge. The old needs to be stripped out, so there has to be a renovation and then a rewiring. What God is saying is that you learned one way to live, you learned one way to talk, you learned one way to act. Now I want you to spit it out, I want to give you a new way. Rejoice in the Lord always, that's new. Don't worry, that's new. Count it all joy, give and it shall be given unto you, study the Word, praising God, speaking in tongues, casting out devils, divine healing: all of these things are new. We are all in the rewiring process. You don't strip all those wires at one time. It is a spiritual process to renovate and rewire.

2. **A Steady Advancement to Follow God's Spiritual Truths.** Being transformed by the renewing of your mind is a steady advancement to follow God's spiritual truths. Notice I use the words "steady advance." You just can't say, "I'm going to learn it all in a week or a month, or year, or fifteen years." I've been at it for fifteen years, and I've just learned enough to realize I have a long way to go. It's a steady advancement to follow God's spiritual truths.

3. **A Continual Ordering of Behavior within the Sphere of the Word.** "BE NOT CONFORMED TO THIS WORLD, BUT BE YE TRANSFORMED BY THE RENEWING OF YOUR MIND." That will enable you to continually order your behavior within the sphere of the Word of God. Any area of life where you can't order your behavior in line with the Bible, means your mind has not been renewed in that area. The old nature is able to take over your mind and your emotions and feelings and dominate you in that area. For example: when anger takes over, Satan begins to reign and rule in your life. This shows us the importance of continually ordering our behavior within the sphere of the Word. It says: "Rejoice in the Lord"; no, it says, "Be depressed by one situation after ano-

ther." Heaviness: do you know what the spirit of heaviness is? He says He'll give you something else — gladness for the spirit of heaviness (depression.) So therefore, it has to be a steady advancement to follow God's spiritual truths. You don't begin to walk in it all at once, but when depression, confusion, frustration, resentment, anger, animosity or anything on this line begins to come your way, just have an honest mind, and say, "Wait a minute now, this is not God. I'm not steadily advancing to follow God's spiritual truths. I was following God and all of a sudden I made a left turn and followed the devil. I'm going to make an about-face and start following God again." Someone says, "When that anger gets hold of me I just can't control it." First of all, that's a bad confession. That shows you have an unrenewed mind. And what you're really saying is that the devil is able to control you. Be honest about it. If you let him take over and you got angry, he controlled you. He pulled your string and you did what he told you to do. You let him put that depression on you, that confusion. Anything you let him put on you, he will. Tell me something good depression does for you. "Why do I have such hard trouble always coming by way?" You probably like pity, you want some sympathy, you're probably being ignored, so you're boing to get a little pampering, and so you do your little things, not realizing that Satan is controlling you. It's amazing how adults in their Christian life still act like little babies. If little babies don't get their way, do you know what they do? They roll on the floor. You know what adults do? They pout? they roll on the floor and pout, and put on a long face. You don't have to ask them if anything is wrong with them (and they want you to ask them), that's why they're showing the long face. If they didn't want you to know, they'd put a smile on it. "GREATER IS HE THAT IS IN YOU THAN HE THAT IS IN THE WORLD." You're "more than a conqueror" through Jesus Christ. If you smile you don't get any attention. If you're smiling everybody just leaves you alone. Steadily, continually ordering your behavior according to the Word, that's the transformed mind. If you can't do this, it means your foundation is improper. The Word of God will pinpoint you. When the pressure comes and you don't have much Word in you, that unrenewed mind comes up. It is not God's will for you to be up and down all the time. God wants you up, but you will have to face it and realize that your mind needs to be transformed by the Word of God.

4. New Mentality that No Longer Judges or Understands as it Once Did. The Word gives you a new mentality. It gives you a mentality of health, of love, of joy, of peace, of victory. You no longer judge or understand as you once did. A report comes back to you about what somebody said about you; boy, with your other mentality you judge them. But now, you know what you do? You say, "Lord God, forgive them." You pray for them. That's a new mentality, that comes from the Word. Your reactions become Word based. The Word says, "BLESSED ARE YOU WHEN YOU ARE REVILED OR PERSECUTED." So when people revile you or persecute you, you just say, "Glory to God, Praise the Lord. Lord, I pray for them. Lord, I just lift them up to you, they have problems." Because, you see, they are being anti-Scriptural. Praise God, I believe God is going to bring a new mentality to His people, a mentality that lines up with the Word of God.

5. A Transformed Mind Gives You Knowledge to Avoid Conformity to this World. Only as your mind is transformed will you have a knowledge to avoid conformity to the world. This is why when the Word is taught it will affect you, because the Word is not teaching from this world but it is teaching from another world, and it will not line up with this world. The gospel is good news, and that good news is not meant to pacify you. the gospel is good news to give you the Truth, so your life can be changed to conform to the Word of God. The Word will enable you to walk in the image of the things of God. That's good news! It gives you a knowledge to avoid conformity. You have the knowledge of the Word that says, "REJOICE IN THE LORD ALWAYS." That revelation of the Word in your heart gives you knowledge to avoid conforming to the world. What does the world do? God says, "BE NOT CONFORMED TO

THIS WORLD." How do many workers act on Monday morning? How do you act? I have knowledge, I don't conform. When troubles come my way, I have the knowledge of God, I count it all joy, I just run and shout. I don't conform to it, I don't yield, I don't fear things that could cause fear in my life. I don't conform to fear. A situation comes to attempt to defeat you, for example —finances. You know how I broke out of poverty? I don't conform to the world. In the world if you get into a situation where you need a hundred dollars and you have fifty dollars, the way to conform is to hold on to that fifty and try to pinch and save. I didn't conform; I gave away the fifty dollars. I have the knowledge of God not to conform to the world system. Don't conform to the world in any way. God's ways are right; man's ways are wrong. The Lord's desire is that His children do things His way. When your mind is transformed, it gives you knowledge to avoid conforming to the world, and then you will cause the power of God to bless you.

6. **Conduct Reflects Pilgrims, Not Citizens of this World.** When you're transformed the conduct reflects that you are a pilgrim, you're just passing through. You represent another kingdom. You know, a man who is raised in China, as he comes to America, it's hard for him to act like us in everything he does. He can't look like us, because he is not American. I can go to China, I can start acting like them, but I can't do it all because I am not Chinese. In the same way, there is no way in the world that I can act like the heathens in the world. I'm a pilgrim, I'm from another world. I'm just passing through this world. I have God living inside of me! When your mind is transformed, then your conduct will reflect that you are a pilgrim, you're not a citizen. I'm not laying up treasures down here. God says if I serve Him, He'll give me everything that I need down here. He says, "I will give you everything you need to get from here to there." I'm not about to waste my time trying to do it, because I am teachable, I'm smart with the ways of God and the Word of God. When you get single-minded upon God and let God move in your life, I guarantee you His Word works. If it doesn't work for you now, it might not work for you when you die, but

God's Word works all the time. If your foundation is proper, then your conduct will reflect it. You'll have the proper knowledge to act like a son of God, heir of God, joint heir with Jesus Christ, rejoicing in the Lord always. When something arises that should worry you, how should a pilgrim act, how should a Christian act? Should they worry? Who worries? The world worries. God says, Don't be conformed to them. If they worry and you worry, you're just like them. Remember that transforming the mind is progressive. Is it easy to stop worrying? I didn't say it was easy, but the Bible says you "CAN DO ALL THINGS THROUGH JESUS CHRIST WHO STRENGTHENS YOU" (Philippians 4:13). Love my neighbors as myself? Impossible! You don't know my neighbor! Well, you don't know God. You can love them. What you're saying is they've done you so many things you don't want to love them, they don't deserve your love. You want to punish them a little bit by giving them a cold shoulder. That's conforming to the world. The heathen like to make people suffer. When you don't treat a brother or sister right, and don't love a neighbor, what you're trying to do is punish them by withholding your love. You're trying to put punishment upon yourself, too. They've embarrassed you or hurt your pride somewhere. But when the mind is transformed by the Word of God, you don't do that, you just love them, praise God, and go on.

7. **A Transformed Mind Knows Howling with the Wolves is Costly.** You go howling with the wolves and you're going to pick up demons. If you are going to slop with the pigs, you're going to pick up demons. What do you mean, "slopping with the pigs"? Getting in the slop pen of worry. Go howling with the wolves with anger, hurt, resentment, bitterness, fear, frustration, confusion, etc. You can't do that, it will always cause you trouble. What do I do, then? Rejoice in the Lord always; it gets easier and easier, the more you walk. You have received the knowledge of God; it is opposite to conformity, so you don't get angry because someone else gets angry. If you feel anger rising up inside of you, walk off somewhere and say, "Jesus, forgive me, I just sinned." Even if others are in the pig-

pen there is no use for you to get in the pigpen with them. Two angry people in the pigpen, both wallowing in the same mud, eating the same slop, anger. You get three or four people together being controlled by fear, they are all slopping in the pigpen of fear, wallowing in fear; and it will kill you! It will take away your joy. This will help you to understand when you're in control, when the devil is in control, or when the Holy Spirit is in control. Any time you come to a situation where something that the world conforms to is controlling you, immediately you can recognize that the Holy Spirit of God is not in control, your unrenewed mind is. Really, Saints, it is no real problem to know what to do and what not to do. The Bible is clear, and plain, and simple. It is just a matter of your making up your mind to be teachable and realize that what God says is what you do every time.

When I come to a red light, I don't have a problem. I just stop. If I see the light turning yellow, I start stopping. I'm teachable. The yellow light says get ready to stop, so I get ready to stop. I'm not going to argue with it. Argue with the light and you will end up getting a ticket. Here is the spiritual application: God says don't worry, so I don't worry. But the world says you have to worry. Read the sixth chapter of Matthew. Whenever you say you have to worry, you are revealing right then that your mind is not renewed with the Word of God. Whenever something comes out and it doesn't line up with the Word of God, you're exposing yourself. You are giving a revelation of your inward man, and really showing your inner self. It is really just a matter of making up your mind that you're going to be faithful to the Lord Jesus Christ and that you're going to believe His Word, that whatever God says to do, simply do it. God says give, I'm going to give. God says rejoice in the Lord always, I'm going to rejoice. God says count it all joy, I'm going to do it. God says don't worry, I'm not going to worry. Any time the enemy tries to make me worry I just say, "Devil, get away from me; I refuse to worry." Remember, I told you this renewal of the mind is progressive. When you first start seeing these things, Saints, if you're not careful it will get heavy for you. You start saying, "Oh, I can't make it." You can't come into all of this over night. Begin now to do your best, then God will make your best better. You will be able to go further. You can't come to a place of perfection over night. We have to have honest minds, be teachable, and realize that our minds have to be transformed to be like Jesus. No one starts at the top of the ladder, we all start at the bottom.

IV.   A POWERFUL MIND: A powerful mind can only be a mind that is renewed with the Word of God.

1. **Casting Down.** II Cor. 10:5 says, "Casting down"; this means "flinging down." The word "casting" means, in Greek, it is like when you see a big black spider. What do you do? You cast it down, you fling it. He says, fling down imaginations and every high thing, every thought that exalteth itself against the knowledge of God. The knowledge of God says don't worry, right? He says, fling down every thought that will exalt itself against the knowledge of God. The knowledge of God says, rejoice in the Lord always. He says cast down imaginations. You see, a thought produces imaginations. Imagination = reasoning, arguments and questions. Imaginations are reasoning.He says, rejoice in the Lord always. He says cast down imaginations. You see, a thought produces imaginations. Imagination = reasonsing, arguments and questions. Imaginations are reasoning. He says cast down every reasoning. Every reasoning, every argument that the man in the world presents to you; they are devices and schemes to attack the Word. So it says cast down all reasoning. "I know that it says to rejoice in the Lord always, but there are certain circumstances that I just can't." That's reasoning; that's argument; that is your argument against the Word of God. That's your argument to justify why you don't obey the Word of God. He says fling down every reasoning, every argument that you have.

2.   **Imaginations.** Reasoning, and questions and arguments are always hostile to the Word. All your reasoning, all your arguments, all your questions are hostile devices and schemes that you are bringing forth to justify why you don't obey the Word. There is no excuse for it. Just make your

decision and stop. The words "casting down" mean wrecking, demolish, put them to the sword, cut them off. God says demolish, cast down, put the sword, cut off, every imagination, every reasoning, every argument, every question, because all of them are hostile devices. It doesn't matter how much you butter it up with your justification, when it contradicts the Word it is hostile, and it must be cast down. Some say, " I just don't believe that." It doesn't make any difference what you believe, if it doesn't line up with the Word, you're wrong, you're disobedient. God isn't wrong, you are wrong, you are the liar. We need to come to the place that we do not question the integrity of the Word of God. We don't reason against it, we don't argue against it, we don't question, we just say, I believe. Now that's faith. Anything else is imagination, reasoning, arguments and discussions. "EXALTETH ITSELF AGAINST THE KNOWLEDGE OF GOD." What do you think about anything that exalteth itself against the knowledge of God? You think that's wise? Anything that I will bring forth or you will bring forth that exalts itself against the knowledge of God, is not wisdom at all, because God's knowledge is pure and perfect. He said, "BRINGING INTO CAPTIVITY EVERY THOUGHT TO THE OBEDIENCE OF CHRIST." Bring them to prison. Bring every thought into captivity through the obedience of the Word. Depending on how much you obey Him, and are faithful, He will bless you because you are His children. Those who are going to receive the fulness of the things of God are beginning to conquer their minds and refuse to come forth with reasoning and arguments and questions about the Word of God.

3.　Thoughts. It says, bring into captivity every thought. What is thought? It's a product of the intelligent mind, a result of thinking. Look what God says. He says fling down, wreck, demolish, put the sword to every imagination, every reasoning, argument, questioning, because it's a hostile device or scheme against the knowledge of God, and bring into captivity, bring into prison, every thought. A thought is the product of the intelligent mind. Every result of your thinking that will contradict the knowledge of God, question God's Word, put it in prison, lock it up and throw the key away. I have people all the time tell me what they think. It's none of my business what they think, in fact I don't want to hear it. Because I don't like them calling my God a liar, because if what they think doesn't line up with the Word, they are calling Him a liar, and He's not a liar. So I know they are; I don't like to talk to liars. Recognize this and realize who you are and what you are. Don't reason with the Word of God, just believe it. Somebody says, I believe this; you say, I believe God! But I've been taught this all my life. I believe God! Well, I think I have a right. I believe God! A dead man doesn't have any rights; he gave them all up. You and I gave up our rights. You do not have a right to question the Word of God.

V.   A DISCIPLINED MIND: Nehemiah 4:6 says, "THE PEOPLE HAD A MIND TO WORK." Study is work. It's easy to watch TV for an hour; you can sit back and watch it for an hour and time just flies, doesn't it? Watch a football game or a basketball game and time just flies. Try studying for an hour. When the program comes on at 7 o'clock just say, OK, I'm going to study for an hour, until 8 o'clock. It's strenuous, and it takes a disciplined mind. You have to have a mind to work, but most Christians don't have a mind to work, not around the Word of God. It requires energy, so most do very little of it. II Tim. 2:15 -- "STUDY TO SHEW THYSELF APPROVED UNTO GOD." Joshua 1:8 says, "THIS BOOK OF THE LAW SHALL NOT DEPART OUT OF THY MOUTH; BUT THOU SHALT MEDITATE (ponder, shew it, mutter) THEREIN DAY AND NIGHT, THAT THOU MAYEST OBSERVE TO DO ACCORDING TO ALL THAT IS WRITTEN THEREIN." God said only as you learn to meditate on His Word day and night will you be able to do all that is written therein. Notice this, "THEN THOU SHALT MAKE THY WAY PROSPEROUS, AND THEN THOU SHALT HAVE GOOD SUCCESS." A disciplined mind gets in the Word, and God says then you will make your way prosperous. What most are trying to do is make their way prosperous before they do the meditating. But the Word says differently!

Psalm 1:1 - 3 "BLESSED IS THE MAN THAT WALK-
ETH NOT IN THE COUNSEL OF THE UNGODLY (the man
that doesn't listen to the advice of the heathen, the sinner),
NOR STANDETH IN THE WAY OF SINNERS, NOR SITTETH
IN THE SEAT OF THE SCORNFUL. BUT HIS DELIGHT IS
IN THE LAW OF THE LORD (the Word of the Lord); AND IN
HIS LAW DOTH HE MEDITATE DAY AND NIGHT. AND HE
SHALL BE LIKE A TREE PLANTED BY THE RIVERS OF
WATER, THAT BRINGETH FORTH HIS FRUIT IN HIS SEA-
SON; HIS LEAF ALSO SHALL NOT WITHER: AND WHAT-
SOEVER HE DOETH SHALL PROSPER," because of medi-
tating His Word both day and night. Let me read Joshua 1:8
the way I read it: "The Word of God shall not depart out of
my mind, out of my mouth, but I shall meditate therein day
and night; then I will observe and be able to do according to all
that is written therein; then I shall make my way prosperous
and then I shall have good success; in everything I put my hand
to, it shall prosper." That's the disciplined mind.

I Peter 1:16 says, "Be ye holy; for I am holy." Have a
sober mind, gird up the loins of your mind, gird up all the
things that will impede your progress with God. God says
gird up the lins of your mind, He says reach down and get
everything out of your way that will impede your progress
from going on with the Lord Jesus Christ.

Philippians 4:7 says, Be anxious about nothing.
Isaiah 26:3 says, He whose mind is stayed upon the Word
shall have perfect peace. He whose mind is stayed upon the
Word; now, Saints that takes a conquered mind. He whose
mind is stayed, is fixed, is aimed upon the Word. When your
mind is on the Word you receive what the Word promises, and
you will be able to hold fast for it, and stick to it, and walk
with it, and therefore receive it.

I believe that the proper foundation is in the process of
being laid. Meditate upon these marks of a proper foundation:
an honest mind, a teachable mind, a transformed mind, a
powerful mind, and a disciplined mind.

OUTLINE ... CHAPTER THREE
Purpose of the Conquest

INTRODUCTION

I.   ERASE SATAN'S PROGRAMMING: Romans 8:7, "Carnal mind is enmity against God." Romans 12:2.

II. DESTROY SATAN'S CONTROL ABILITY: Philippians 4:8.

III. ESTABLISH A COMMUNICATION LANGUAGE: John 16:13, "Spirit of truth." Speaks in line with Word.

IV. INCREASE YOUR ABILITY TO OBEY THE WORD OF GOD: James 2:17, "Faith, if it hath not works, is dead, being alone." Prevents manifestations.

V.   FREE FROM CONDEMNATION Romans 8:1, "Who walk not after the flesh, but after the Spirit." Satan condemns but God convicts.

VI. ELIMINATE DEMON EFFECTIVENESS: The unrenewed mind is an open door.

VII. DECREASE THE POSSIBILITY OF DECEPTION: Galatians 3:1, "O foolish, who hath bewitched you, that ye should not obey the truth (word)." II Peter 2:19, "For of whom a man is overcome, of the same is he brought in bondage." II Peter 2:2, "Many shall follow their ways."

VIII. **INCREASE GUIDANCE:** II Peter 2:9, "The Lord knows how to deliver the Godly out of temptations."

IX. **PROPER JUDGMENTS:** I Corinthians 2:15, "He that is spiritual judgeth all things, yet he himself is judged of no man."

Word, not senses, as to who you are.

X. **ENABLE YOU TO ENDURE BOMBARDMENT OF MIND:** Hebrews 12: 3, "Consider him that endured such opposition and hostility, so that you may not grow weary, exhausted, losing heart and fainting in your mind."

By devil, demons, people and situations.

XI. **PREVENT COUNTERFEITS OF FAITH:** Romans 10:10, "Confess with your mouth and believe in your heart."

XII. **DEFEAT FEAR IN SOULISH REALM:**
Fear is in the soul and not the spirit. II Corinthians 5:17.

XIII. **VOID LAW OF OLD ATTRACTIONS:** - Mind, desires, lusts, etc. New view of all.

XIV. **ESTABLISH A TEACHABLE MIND TO BIBLE CONCEPTS:**
Bring understanding and acceptance of the Word of God.

XV. **INCREASE POSSIBILITY OF PROSPERITY:**
1. Spiritually
2. Physically
3. Finanacially
4. Relationships

XVI. **BIRTH STRONG ASSURANCE AND CONFIDENCE**

CHAPTER THREE
Purpose of the Conquest

INTRODUCTION: As we study the purpose of the conquest I want you to notice a verse of Scripture. This is God's Word to you. Romans 12:2 is not a man talking to you, is not just an Apostle. The Bible is God Himself speaking directly to you. I want you to receive this as if God were standing here speaking directly to you. God said He put His Word above His name (Psalm 138:2). Romans 12:2 is God speaking to you as you read this book. This is what God is saying to His people. "AND BE NOT CONFORMED TO THIS WORLD, BUT BE YE TRANSFORMED BY THE RENEWING OF YOUR MIND, THAT YOU MAY PROVE WHAT IS THAT GOOD, AND ACCEPTABLE, AND PERFECT, WILL OF GOD." God says don't be conformed to this world but be transformed by the renewal of your mind. Why? That you may prove to yourself and to the world, that you may demonstrate what is the good, acceptable, and perfect, will of God. There is no way we can prove what is the good, acceptable, and perfect, will of God for our lives unless we are obedient to God. If you can prove it, then God is wrong. He set a condition for you to prove what is the good, acceptable, and perfect will of God. You are not to be conformed to this world. You are not to be like them. You are not to think like them, not to talk like them, not to walk like them, because God says you are now a citizen of another world. "You are now My ambassador in this world to the people of this world." The Lord says, "I've chosen you and elected you, called you out and ordained you, and equipped you, that you might represent Me here in this world. I have chosen you to represent heaven. I have chosen you to represent the godly kind of life. I have not chosen you to represent heaven part of the time, and hell part of the time, and the world part of the time. I have not chosen you to talk heaven part of the time, and talk hell part of the time, and talk the world part of the time. I have not chosen you to live heavenly part of the time and live worldly part of the time." He said, "I've called you to not be conformed to the world but to be transformed by the renewing of your mind and so that you can prove what is the good and acceptable, and perfect will of God." When you are reading the Bible you're not reading a book from man. Don't read it like you read a history book, or science book, or a comic book. We've read so long we just read and don't think much about it. So many times we forget that when we read the Bible, we are reading the Word of God directly to you and me. Many people say, "Well, Brother Willis, if an angel would appear to me I could obey what he said." If you won't obey the Word of God Himself, you won't obey His angel. If you can't believe God Himself, you can't believe His angel, you can't believe anything. If you are in that situation, you need to say, "God, forgive me. I just read it in a hurry, God, and said 'He doesn't really mean that' (but He said what He meant)." It is the Word of God, the eternal Word of God. Never doubt the integrity of God's Word. You will never prove the good, acceptable, perfect will of God, never walk in the fullness of the things of God, unless you begin to realize that the Word of God is God speaking directly to you. God said rejoice in the Lord always (Philippians 4:4). You don't have the right to decide if you want to do it or not. You gave up that right when you accepted Jesus as your Saviour. The only thing that we are responsible to do now is read the Word, believe it, and do it. It is sin to read it and not do it. We should say, "I am about to read what God is telling me to do. I'm going to read it and believe God is speaking to me, and as I read it realize I'm accountable to do it." This is one of the main purposes of the conquest of the mind, that your mind begins to accept that the Bible is not just another book. It is not something you have the right to accept or reject, or debate. But when you begin to read it, say, "When I read this God is speaking to me and from that moment on I'm accountable to obey it." It doesn't make any difference what you think, because your thinking is wrong. You don't have the right to say, "I can't do what the Word of God asks of me." "I CAN DO ALL THINGS THROUGH JESUS CHRIST WHO STRENGTHENS ME." (Philippians 4:13) You don't have a right to say, "I can't do it." You don't have the right to say, "I can't stand on the Word of God," because the Word of God says (in I John 4:4), "GREATER IS HE THAT IS IN YOU THAN HE THAT IS IN THE WORLD." I'm encouraging you right now to realize this great truth. You pick up a telephone book and find the number and then dial it. You don't argue with it, you just dial it, proving that you believe it. But when you come to the Word of God and read it, you debate it. This is one of the reasons the renewing of the mind is so important, because until the person's mind is renewed he will not begin to accept God's Word as being directly to him.

God has commissioned you and me to bring our minds under control of the Word of God and submit them to the control of the Holy Spirit of the Living God, that we might live and walk in the victory that God has ordained before the foundation of the world. You and I are not just children of man, we are children of God, and God actually lives in us in the presence of Jesus Christ, His Son, enabling us to have our minds renewed, to talk different, walk different, think different, and act different in everything.

I.   ERASE SATAN'S PROGRAMMING. Now one of the purposes of this reprogramming is to ERASE SATAN'S PRO-GRAMMING. Romans 8:7, "THE CARNAL MIND IS ENMITY AGAINST GOD." Romans 12:2 must come into existence if you are going to prove what is the good, and acceptable, and perfect, will of God. You will never find it for your life unless your mind is renewed by the Word of God. The carnal mind, the fleshly mind, the earthly mind, is enmity to God. The first time I read Philippians 4:4 where it says "REJOICE IN THE LORD ALWAYS," my mind was at enmity against God. Any time your mind will not accept the Word of God, and wants to argue with it and debate it and discuss it and water it down, that means your mind is the enemy of God, and it ought not be that way. God has placed His mighty Spirit in you to help you endure. We have to erase Satan's programming. Since you and I were born we've been programmed by this world. Our mind is like a computer and the devil is the god of this world, and he's made sure that what you have in your mind will not line up with the Word of God. He's placed all the garbage of doubt, fear, and worry in your mind so that you will not accept the Word of God. If your mind is renewed by the Word of God it will erase the devil's programming. I was programmed by the world and by the devil to be sick; I erased it. God says by the stripes of Jesus you were healed at Calvary (Isaiah 53:4,5). But the unrenewed mind says, I don't understand that. Then you go into logic and reason. He didn't ask you to understand it, He asked you to believe it, and then your understanding will come. The unrenewed mind says, "I know what the Bible says, but I just can't see it that way" (ungodly mind). That's the kind of mind that is talking devil talk. That's a mind which has enough meanness and devilness in it that it will contradict and question the integrity of God's Word every time. Any time your mind controls your mouth and your mouth will question the Word of God, then you will be speaking directly against God. You will be questioning God's integrity. You are saying, "God, I think you made a mistake when you wrote that." You are saying, "God, I think you're demanding too much of me." You are saying, "God, I think you're requiring too much of me." I want you to know that the Word of God will erase all that old programming and you will get to the place where you will say, "God, I believe, so I thereby receive. Be it unto me, Lord God, according to thy Word." Mary, the mother of Jesus, knew the laws of Genesis; she knew it took a man and a woman to produce life. An angel of God came and told her, "You're going to have a Son and His name shall be called Jesus, and no man is going to touch you." He is going to be born of God. All of her training, everything she knew, questioned these words of the angel, because she asked the question, how! How can this be so? Mary finally said, in Luke 1:38, "BE IT UNTO ME ACCORDING TO THY WORD." She said, "With my mind I cannot perceive how I can have a son without a man. With my mind I know that the laws of nature say no, it's impossible; but, God, You said it and I believe it." That's where God wants you and me to come, to the place we read it and say, "God, You said it, I believe it. You said by the stripes of Jesus I was healed at Calvary, so I am." But your body says you're not. You know the laws of sickness and disease; it's time for you to say, "Be it unto me according to thy Word, God," not be it unto me according to the laws of the body. Not according to the laws of sickness and disease, but be it unto me according to thy Word. This will erase Satan's programming. The only thing that can erase it is for you to get busy. And it will be a battle because you have lived a certain way all your life. You thought a certain way all your life; you think that has been the right way. Then you begin to read the Bible and you hear someone preaching the truth of the Bible, and your mind rebels. Your mind wants to go its own way. You want to do your own thing. But Christ says that any man who does not forsake all and follow Him is not worthy of the kingdom of God. You better forsake all and follow Him.

II. DESTROY SATAN'S CONTROL ABILITY. Saints, the purpose of the conquest of the mind is so that you can DESTROY SATAN'S CONTROL ABILITY THROUGH PRIOR PROGRAMMING AND SENSE STIMULATION. So you want to destroy his ability to control you. Do you know Satan can still control most people with anger? Do you know that he can use fear today and shake up most Christians? He can stimulate them with a mere accident. He can stimulate them with the thought of the loss of a job and take them over and cause them to begin to speak death and think death. He can stimulate them by having somebody say something against them that touches their feelings and causes them to get angry. He can stimulate them with frustration and confusion, and thereby control them. But saints of God, you have the power in you to destroy Satan's ability to control you. I John 4:4 says that, "GREATER IS HE THAT IS IN YOU THAN HE THAT IS IN THE WORLD." Philippians 4:8 says that you and should think on only those things that are good, just, pure, lovely, honest, and of a good report. Satan can put other thoughts in your mind to stimulate you. He can stimulate you with lust by your looking at a beautiful home. There are more things to lust after besides men and women.

When the mind is under the control of the Word of God and the blood of Jesus, then you destroy Satan's control ability. He can no longer control your life. Your mind is now reprogrammed by the Word of God and now submitted to the Word of God, and the Word of God is now the dominating factor of your life. The Word of God is now King, and to anything that comes to your mind that contradicts the King, you just say, "No. I bow, King Jesus, to Your Word. You have decreed it, so shall it be in my life. You have decreed, King Jesus, that I shall rejoice in the Lord always, so shall it be. You have decreed in Your Word, King Jesus, that by Your stripes I was healed at Calvary, so be it unto me. You have decreed in Your Word that I should not worry, to take no thought for tomorrow (Matthew 6:25 - 34), so be it, King Jesus. Thou art King of Kings and Lord of Lords. Thy Word is true, so be it unto me. I refuse to worry." Have you rebelled against worry yet? Have you decreed and said, "I will not worry?" God tells you not to worry. Oh! He doesn't mean that! Yes, He does; you just don't want to do it. Get your mind to the place where you can destroy Satan's hold. He cannot dominate you any more. Confusion cannot dominate you any more; depression cannot dominate you any more; frustration, anger, insecurity, inferiority cannot dominate you any more. Self pity cannot dominate you any more, because the Word is now the dominating factor in your life. You now bow to the truth of the Word of God, and the Word of God, and the Word of God has the absolute rulership in your life. You destroyed Satan's hold. You can do it, because He that is in you is greater than he that is in the world. You can do it; it's your mind; you can bring it under the authority of the Word of God. Your mind is a vessel for the Holy Spirit of God to speak to you and lead and guide you into all truth (John 16:13).

III. ESTABLISH A COMMUNICATION LANGUAGE. Another purpose of the conquest of the mind is to ESTABLISH A COMMUNICATION LANGUAGE. The Bible is the language of God, and as long as your mind is filled with the language of the world, the language of society, then you don't have the language for the Holy Spirit of God to communicate the truth to you. God will always speak to you in line with His Word. I woke up one morning with one word in my mind, the word "hasten." I remembered a Scripture in Jeremiah 1:12, which says, "I WILL HASTEN MY WORD TO PERFORM IT." I'd just picked up that one word. I woke up and there it was, "hasten," in Jeremiah 1:12, because I know God's language says I will hasten My Word to perform it. So God spoke to me that morning and said, "Son, I will hasten My Word to perform it," because I know the language of God, and the language of God has become my communication channel. John 16:13, "THE SPIRIT OF TRUTH WILL GUIDE YOU INTO ALL TRUTH." The Spirit of Truth Who lives in you is going to guide you into all truth. He is always going to speak in line with the Word of God. If you do not have the vocabulary of God, you do not have a communication channel for God to speak to you as much as He wants to. God breaks through the language barriers to speak to you in many ways. But there will be more communication when you learn His Word. That's why your mind must be renewed, so you will establish a language of communication. It enables God to speak to you much more. He gave me a word of encouragement that morning. He said, "I hasten My Word to perform it." If you know a language and you just hear a part of a conversation, many times you can understand it. If you had not known that Scripture and you woke up this morning with the word "hasten" in you, you would have been pondering all day long -- hasten, hasten. He wants me to do something. Oh, what am I going to do? But if you have His language you will know He was saying, "I hasten to perform My Word; I will make My Word real to you. I will manifest My Word unto you." So another purpose of conquest is to establish a communication language. That's why it says don't be conformed to this world; because your mind is so conformed to the world that you must have it renewed, transformed by the renewal of the Word of God. Therefore, unless you get more of God's vocabulary in your mind, the Holy Spirit doesn't have enough language to speak to you, because He's going to speak to you in line with the Word of God. You say, "but couldn't He speak to me in the language that I'm talking?" Sure He can, He does sometimes, but I'll tell you what I found out, Saints. The more of His language I know, the more He talks. He spoke to me in what I call old country boy language so I could understand Him. He just told me one time, "You're just scared." He spoke to me so I could understand, "You're scared." Now I said, "God, I'm not scared of anything." He said, "Yes, you are; you're scared of what people might say about you." And I was, so I went out and I bought a Cadillac. I had to break that spirit of what people thought about me. I broke it, and you have to break it. You have to start with the communication language. Now, He'll talk to you in normal language, but His Word is going to speak to you most of the time.

IV.   INCREASE YOUR ABILITY TO OBEY THE WORD OF GOD. Another purpose of the conquest of the mind is that it will INCREASE YOUR ABILITY TO OBEY THE WORD OF GOD. James 2:17 says, "FAITH, IF IT HATH NOT WORKS, IS DEAD, BEING ALONE." The reason why so many times you can't obey the Word of God and can't follow through with it is because your mind has not been renewed by the Word of God. God will give you some instructions that are so peculiar, if you don't know the Word of God you will not be able to obey them. If you don't know how to recognize His voice, you can't obey it.

I remember one time about a year ago He told me to lie down; therefore, I lay down. He told me, "You lie down; you get on your face." I was standing on the platform. What will people say? That's their problem. Philippians 4:8 says only think on things that are pure, just, honest, holy, lovely, and of good report. When I fell down they should just think Bible. When I fell on the floor, if anybody thought anything wrongly about it, they were wrong. People always say, what do you mean, Philippians 4:8? I always keep saying, sometimes you think on those things, or whenever you want to you're thinking on the things that are good, just, holy, pure, lovely and of good report; it didn't say that. You get your mind renewed with the Word of God. He says in James 1:2, "COUNT IT ALL JOY WHEN YE FALL INTO DIVERS TEMPTATIONS." What do you do when some of the problems come your way? If you do anything besides James 1:2 you aren't acting Bible, you are sinning. "But I'm just a baby." He doesn't say in James 1:2 everybody but babies count it all joy. "But I did it for a while, but I fell. What do I do?" Repent! Say, "Oh, God, I fell; I missed you, Lord, forgive me; but Lord, I'm coming back. I'm coming back to the fulness of it." You will have to destroy Satan's control ability, and then establish a communication language, and through the renewal of your mind you will increase your ability to obey the Word of God. I know that you desire to obey God's Word.

I will give you a good example: Malachi 3:10, "BRING YE ALL THE TITHES INTO THE STOREHOUSE." People who can't obey it, I've never heard one of them yet who didn't do it and admitted they were sinning; they always had to justify it. Some of you who are not doing it are justifying it. What you are doing, you're arguing with the Scriptures. You are trying to debate the Word of God and trying to prove that you are right. That proves that your mind is unrenewed, you are in bad shape. Any mind that thinks what they think is above the Word of God, is in bad shape and is unrenewed. The enemy has control over you, because the mind is controlled by the enemy when it will not accept the Word of God. It will argue with the Word of God. But God is growing up a people and bringing them to the place where they are going to say, "God, You said it and I believe it." It just takes the ability to read, the ability to hear, then it takes the ability to say, "I'm going to do what God says." Simple and clear, but not natural. Rejoice in the Lord always is not natural; don't worry is not natural. God's Word tells you to do supernatural things. so increase your ability to obey the Word of God.

If you don't obey the Word of God, you're going to prevent many of your manifestations. Many of you have things by faith. You received them by faith and you're holding and waiting. But a lot of times, because of disobedience to the Word of God, you are preventing God from manifesting the thing for you. A good example is: Are you rejoicing in the Lord always? Many times when things get real tough, what do you do? Obey the Word or disobey the Word? You will be amazed at how many things come through when you keep obeying the Word. If you don't obey the Word, you prevent God from manifesting that thing. You put the stopper in the faucet.

V. **FREES YOU FROM CONDEMNATION:** Here's another purpose of the conquest of the mind: IT FREES YOU FROM CONDEMNATION. Romans 8:1 says, "THERE IS THERE-FORE NOW NO CONDEMNATION TO THEM WHICH ARE IN CHRIST JESUS, WHO WALK NOT AFTER THE FLESH, BUT AFTER THE SPIRIT." A lot of Christians quote this Scripture that there is no condemnation to those that are in Christ Jesus. If individuals don't want to obey the Word of God as it is preached to them, they say, "You're putting me under condemnation." The Word of God is not putting you under condemnation, your disobedience is putting you under condemnation, you opened the door for the devil to put you under condemnation.

SATAN CONDEMNS, BUT GOD CONVICTS. Many times the reason why people are under condemnation is GOD CONVICTED THEM TO DO IT, AND THEY DISOBEYED HIM; then they opened the door for the devil to condemn them. God says, "HE WHO PUTS HIS HAND TO THE PLOW AND LOOKS BACK, IS NOT FIT FOR THE KINGDOM OF GOD" (Luke 9:62). So before you get your hand set on the plow real good, you better consider. I've seen many put their hand to the plow and then turn back and think everything is still all right. But according to the Bible they are in bad shape. God is the one Who said in Luke 10:62 that he who puts his hand to the plow and looks back is not worthy of God.

The blessings of God come as your mind is renewed by the Word of God. What will hinder you from receiving the blessing, is you not obeying the Word of God, and you get your-self under condemnation. There is no condemnation to those in Christ Jesus if you walk after the Spirit. If you don't obey the Word of God, you're in Christ Jesus, but because of your dis-

64

obedience to the Scripture you opened the door for the devil to put you under condemnation. He'll bombard you and beat you down and keep you down for as long as you let him. This is why this study guide on the conquest of the mind -- to help you realize that when you get your mind conquered, it will free you from condemnation. How? Because you will obey the Word. When the conviction inside gets hold of you, you will say, "Lord, I'm going to do it."

You know, Saints, when I started speaking in tongues, I didn't want to teach about "tongues." But I knew that speaking in tongues was real and I knew I put my hands to the plow when I started speaking in tongues, and I knew if I looked back I wouldn't be worthy, so I just kept speaking in tongues and kept plowing. Many times I tried to cancel the insurance, and throw all the medicines away. The devil tried many times to make me go back. But I said, "God, I have my hand to the plow. God, you said if a man puts his hand to the plow and looks back, he's not worthy. Father God, I'm worthy. God, if I go back I'm going to drag the plow with me." The only way you and I can be bold in God is to permit the Holy Spirit of God, through the Word of God, to renew our minds to it can expose all of the things of the old life so that we can go on with God. This is the desire of my heart, and I know it is the desire of your heart. I know that anyone who would pick up a book like this desires to go on with God.

VI. **IT ELIMINATES DEMON EFFECTIVENESS.** Here is another benefit of the conquest of the mind. It ELIMINATES DEMON EFFECTIVENESS, as the unrenewed mind is an open door. If your mind is not renewed with the Word of God, and you don't understand the Word of God and you're not meditating and studying the Word of God, you are an open door for demonic influence. The demons of hurt can come back and hurt you. Unless your mind gets renewed with the Word of God, you'll find yourself in the situation, and later on that demon of hurt will come back. That old demon of remembrance will remind you of all the hurt that you had. The enemy keeps on working with you through fear, or frustration, or confusion, or disappointment, or hate, or resentment or rebellion, or envy, or anger, or animosity, or jealousy, etc. Until your mind gets renewed, the devil keeps you going in cycles in these things. He works awhile with anger, and awhile with frustration, and awhile with insecurity. Beloved, there is victory in Jesus for you through the renewal of the mind. You cannot be under condemnation when you have victory over those areas. But, you see, it can't come to pass until you and I accept the Word of God as God's Word and make up our minds that we're going to obey that Word of God regardless. Unless you do it you are green pastures for the demons, you are opening the door for him. Whatever area you have been having difficulty in, you need to realize that Satan has a strong hold on you. If it's fear, if it's anger, if it's worry, if it's hurt, if it's resentment, if it's evil thoughts, or if it's feeling insecure and inadequate, then you need to realize why Satan has a strong hold. Then take the Scriptures, the Word of God, that tell you who you are -- you are a conqueror, an overcomer, you can do all things, He that is in you is greater than he that is in the world. And Saints, you begin to say it and say it, and say it until the Word of God begins to work down inside of you, and begins to come alive and rejects all that disagrees with the Scriptures. Then you begin to walk in the victory that God has ordained for you. You just rise up, beloved saints of God, and come against the enemy; you don't have to live your lives under that oppression. Make up your mind that He that is in you is greater than he that is in the world. You keep on planting the Word in your mind. If you've been failing one time after another, make up your mind that you are not a failure. The Word of God doesn't say you are a failure, the Word of God says you're a conqueror. The Word of God says you're an overcomer. The Word of God says the love of God is shed abroad in your heart. The Word of God says the joy of the Lord is your strength. The Word of God says that the peace that surpasses all understanding is yours. Therefore, Saints, as you begin to get hold of it and get your mind renewed, one of the purposes of the conquest of the mind is you ELIMINATE DEMON EFFECTIVENESS. You will come to the point you can spot them. You can walk in victory 365 days a year because Jesus is Lord of your life. Salvation is for the spirit, you have the Baptism of the Holy Spirit, and you have power. You need to walk in the fullness of Who is in you and get your mind renewed. Saturate yourself with the Word; it will set you free from condemnation and eliminate demon effectiveness.

VII. DECREASE THE POSSIBLITY OF DECEPTION.

Another purpose is that it DECREASES THE POSSIBLITY OF DECEPTION. When your mind is renewed by the Word of God you have so much Word in your mind that every time the devil comes against you, you quote a Scripture back at him. A knowledge of the Word of God will decrease the possiblity of deception, as you get your mind renewed with that Word. Galatians 3:1 says, "O FOOLISH GALATIANS (foolish charismatics), WHO HATH BEWITCHED YOU (who put a spell on you), THAT YE SHOULD NOT OBEY THE TRUTH (the Word)?" If you don't obey the Word you have a spell put on you. The devil has put a spell on you, bewitched you. He's made you think you don't have to do that. He pulled the blinders over your eyes so much that you can argue with the Word of God and still think that you are all right. What kind of spell has been put on you that you can read the Word of God where it says rejoice in the Lord always, and yet the spell is so strong that you don't believe what God says? Who's bewitched you? Who's deceived you? You have a spell cast on you. The powers of darkness have put a spell on you. The devil, through his demons, put a curse on you because you would not accept that Word. Who's bewitched you and made you think that by the stripes of Jesus you were not healed at Calvary? Who's bewitched you and put a spell on you and made you think you can't be healed? That's a spell. The devil has put a spell on you, put a curse on you, set the blinders over your eyes. You read the Word of God: by His stripes I'm healed (Isaiah 53:4,5; I Peter 2:24). "Well, it says that, but it doesn't really mean that." That's blindness. How can you do that as a Christian? The only way you can do that as a Christian is that you have a spell put on you.

The Word of God says in II Timothy 1:7, "GOD HAS NOT GIVEN US THE SPIRIT OF FEAR, BUT OF POWER, AND OF LOVE, AND OF A SOUND MIND." Who's bewitched you and made you think that it is all right for you to still be in fear? You need to have a spell put on you by the Word. II Peter 2:19 - "FOR OF WHOM A MAN IS OVERCOME, OF THE SAME IS HE BROUGHT IN BONDAGE." If you're overcome be fear then you are overcome by Satan, you are under bondage to the enemy. The reason this happens is because the mind is not renewed. If your mind is not overcome and renewed by the Word of God, and anger overcomes you. then where is anger from? The devil! Therefore, you are brought under the bondage of Satan. You are under bondage to that anger, you are under bondage to that fear; it is your master. You are under bondage to worry. A spell has been cast upon you. You think it is all right to worry, so you let worry begin to take over in your life. But praise God, Jesus gave you victory. II Peter 2:2 talks about the false prophets and the false teachers and it says, "MANY SHALL FOLLOW THEIR WAYS." Romans 13:8 says, "OWE NO MAN ANY THING, BUT TO LOVE ONE ANOTHER." You know a lot of people can't believe that? They've been bewitched. You mean there are people who can't believe God's Word? They are bewitched, that's what the Bible says. Any time you can't believe that Word of God, something is wrong; there is some power or some force working mightier in you and with you, causing you not to believe the Word of God. I refuse to be bewitched. I refuse to let a spell be cast on me and make me doubt the Word of God. Romans 13:8 says, "OWE NO MAN ANY THING, BUT TO LOVE ONE AN- OTHER." I'm talking about Christians, Holy Spirit filled Christians. They get bewitched, a spell is cast upon them, and they rationalize the Word of God. They never say it's wrong, but they tell you how to interpret it. What they need to do is read it, and normally it will interpret itself.

VIII. **INCREASES GUIDANCE.** This is another purpose
of the renewal of the mind. II Peter 2:9 says, "THE LORD
KNOWETH HOW TO DELIVER THE GODLY OUT OF TEMP-
TATIONS." That is guidance. As your mind is renewed by the
Word of God and you come to a deeper understanding of the
Word of God, you will receive more from God. Meditate on
it, and as you begin to learn the mind of God, you place your-
self in a position where God can lead you and guide you more.
The more you know the Word, the more you submit to it,
the more you are committed to it. Then you refuse to let the
devil put a spell on you and tie you up. As you plant the
Word of God in your heart, the Holy Spirit of God will begin to guide you and lead you into the beautiful truth of
God's plan for your life, which is abundance in every area.

IX. **PROPER JUDGMENTS:** The Word of God determines
as to who you are, what to do, blessings, etc., not the senses.
I Corinthians 2:15 says, "HE THAT IS SPIRITUAL JUDG-
ETH ALL THINGS, YET HE HIMSELF IS JUDGED OF NO
MAN." When your mind is renewed by the Word of God,
you have proper judgment. You will not judge things by your
senses: by what you see, or what you feel, or what you hear,
or your taste or your touch. You will judge everything by
the Word of God. When you judge it by the Word of God,
then you have proper judgment. If you judge your body when
it is hurting, by your senses, then you will judge it correctly
as far as the world is concerned. Only as your mind is renewed
by the Word of God, can you judge your body properly. When
pain is in my body, I have to make a judgment. I have to make
a quality decision according to the Word or according to my
senses. Now my senses tell me that my body is sick, but the
Word tells me that my body is healed. When my mind is renewed by the Word of God I can then make a proper Biblical
judgment and pronounce my body as healed and whole according to the Word of God. If I make judgment according to my

senses, according to the way I feel, then I would judge my body to be sick according to the world's standard. When your mind is renewed by the Word of God, you always judge your body to be healed. "By the stripes of Jesus I was healed at Calvary." I'm not trying to get saved any more; I am saved. I'm not trying to get healed any more; I AM HEALED. Many times my body tries to prove to me that I am not healed. It tries to dispute the Word of God that says that Jesus took my sicknesses and my infirmities. And when my body disputes the Word of God and argues with the Word of God, then I have to make a judgment. I always judge according to the Word and, therefore, I judge my body to be healed. If your mind is not renewed by the Word of God, you are unable to make a proper judgment about your health, and since you can't make this judgment in line with the Word of God, the door is open to Satan to continually bombard your body with sickness and disease. You must come to the place where you tell Satan, "I want you to know I am healed. I was healed at Calvary according to the Word of God. According to my senses, my feelings, I'm sick; but according to the Word, I'm healed." I have to make a choice. When your mind is renewed by the Word of God there is no problem at all to make the correct choice, the proper judgment: that is, to praise God you are healed. Then your body stays healed and stays healthy and stays in line with the Word of God.

Learn how to make the proper judgment about your finances. Learn how to make the proper judgment about living in victory every day. I live in victory every day. Sometimes circumstances and situations come up that tell me I am not living in victory, but I always make the proper judgment because my mind has been renewed by the Word of God. The circumstances can look dark, the problem can look difficult, the mountain can look high; but I don't go by the mountain, I don't go by the darkness of the problem, I don't go by the difficulty of a situation, because my mind has been renewed by the Word of God, that "HE THAT IS IN ME IS GREATER THAN HE THAT IS IN THE WORLD"; that I am "MORE THAN A CONQUEROR THROUGH CHRIST JESUS." I always make the proper judgment and I judge that I have victory over those circumstances and those situations. When your mind is not renewed by the Word of God, you are double-minded. Sometimes you say you're healed and sometimes you say that you're not. Sometimes you say you are prosperous and sometimes you say that you are not prosperous. **Proper judgment is always based upon the Word of God.** You must always judge everything correctly. The Word is the pure truth. Anything that will change is not really truth. You can have pain in your body and that pain can say, I'm true. The pain may leave, therefore it is not really truth; it changed. Truth never changes. The Word of God says, by the stripes of Jesus you're healed, and it never, never changes. The proper way for you to evaluate and consider these things is in line with something that never changes. The Word of God never changes. Your check book may say five dollars; it may tell you, "I'm the truth," but you can change it just by writing a check. Anything that can be changed is not pure truth. Truth never changes. Make a valued judgment, either according to the Word or according to what you see, feel, hear, taste or touch. A person cannot do that until his mind is renewed by the Word of God. Some of you may have difficulty saying that you're healed when your body hurts. I can understand why: it is because your mind is not renewed by the Word of God.

A few years ago I had difficulty saying my body was healed, when it hurt. But I don't have any difficulty at all now. It would be harder for me to say that I'm sick than for a man whose mind is not renewed by the Word of God. It's impossible for me to violate the law of the Word of God, because God's Word says by the stripes of Jesus I was healed at Calvary. Only renewed minds can make proper judgments

71

in these areas. We read in I Corinthians 2:15, "HE THAT IS SPIRITUAL (he that is educated in the Word of God, led by the Spirit of God, who obeys the Word of God) JUDGETH ALL THINGS." I judge the pain in my body, I judge it as from the devil. "YET HE HIMSELF IS JUDGED OF NO MAN." If you are moving in the Word of God, no man will be able to judge you for anything you have done, because you will judge yourself before he does. If someone says, "Brother Willis, you sinned; you got angry," they didn't judge me. I already judged myself; the minute I got angry I said, "Lord Jesus Christ, forgive me, I have sinned." I judge my body, I judge it healed according to the Word of God. I judge my finances; I judge my bank account to be filled according to the Word. Sometimes my bank account tells me something else. It says, "You are not prosperous." I make proper judgment, that "THE BLESSING OF THE LORD, IT MAKETH RICH, AND HE ADDETH NO SORROW WITH IT." (Proverbs 10:22) You can't do this unless your mind has been renewed by the Word of God. You will revert back to the flesh. Or sometimes you will be confessing the Word and sometimes you will be confessing something else. Learn to be consistent—believe the Word of God every time.

X. IT ENABLES YOU TO ENDURE BOMBARDMENT OF THE MIND, by the devil, demons, people and situations. If your mind is not renewed by the Word of God, the devil will bombard you, the demons will bombard you, people will bombard you, and circumstances and situations will put so much pressure on you, and you will not be able to stand. Hebrews 12:3 says, "FOR CONSIDER HIM THAT ENDURED SUCH CONTRADICTION OF SINNERS AGAINST HIMSELF, LEST YE BE WEARIED AND FAINT IN YOUR MINDS." Your mind must be renewed by the Word of God, you must learn the Word and how to hold to the Word, because if your mind is not renewed by the Word of God the devil and his demons will come against you and cause you to be

72

defeated. If your mind is renewed by the Word of God, the devil and the demons, people, circumstances and situations can put pressure on you, and you make the proper judgment. You say, "Praise God, He that is in me is greater than he that is in the world; I'm more than a conqueror in Christ Jesus. I can do all things through Jesus Christ who strengthens me. Not by might, and not by power, but by the Spirit." He says in Luke 10:19, "BEHOLD, I GIVE UNTO YOU POWER TO TREAD ON SERPENTS AND SCORPIONS, AND OVER ALL THE POWER OF THE ENEMY: AND NOTHING SHALL BY ANY MEANS HURT YOU."

It is only as your mind is renewed (conquered) that you will be able to endure that bombardment. Have you observed when you believe God for something how your mind gets bombarded? When you are believing God for a healing and the devil is attacking your body? When you are believing God for your family to be in harmony, be flowing together, then all kinds of problems are stirring up and the devil bombards your mind. When your mind is renewed by the Word of God, situations say you can't make it and you just raise your hands and smile and say, "The joy of the Lord is my strength. He that is in me is greater than he that is in the world. I'm more than a conqueror through Christ Jesus." But, you see, if your mind is not renewed by the Word of God you cannot do that. When all that trouble is going on you grow weary, exhausted, and you lose heart and faint in your mind. Your mind can't stand the pressure. The mind must be renewed by the Word of God to be able to stand the pressure that the devil puts upon you. So many times you're trying to fight the devil without using the Word. The Word is your sword. The only way you can whip the devil is to quote Scriptures. Hold fast to that Scripture. How did Jesus defeat him? He said, "It is written." When troubles are coming against you, say, "It is written: He that is in me is greater than he that is in the world." When people are ridiculing you and mocking you, you say, "It is written: blessed are you when you're persecuted and reviled for my name's sake." Quote the Scripture and stand on it. State your position, state what you believe, and let that always be the Word of God. Don't state the situation, don't state what the individual has said. Don't state the way you feel. Don't state the way things look. State only the Word of God. A mind that is not renewed by the Word has difficulty doing i'. The pressure gets so high, they stay in their feelings. Only renewed minds can endure the bombardment of the enemy.

The way to be able to walk in victory is to bring our minds under the control of the Word of God. Many times my mind tries to run off somewhere. My mind reacts quicker to a bad thought than my hand does to a hot fire. When your hand touches something hot, what do you do? Well, be smart with your mind. When it thinks on something that doesn't line up with Philippians 4:8, cast it off. Examine your thoughts. When you touch something hot with your hand, does it take you long to examine it? Certainly not! In the same way, when your mind wanders to something that doesn't line up with Philippians 4:8, on something that is not good, just, holy, pure, lovely, honest and of good report, examine it real good. If it doesn't fit your Bible, get your mind off of it. It's your mind, just like your hand. If somebody tries to hold your hand on something hot, you jerk your hand away! But you'll let your mind stay on garbage, and sit there and burn. When the mind gets on a thought that will harm them, you know what most people do? They hold on to it. Drop it! It's hot, it's burning you. It's hurting you. Examine it quickly. The thought of discouragement, depression, loneliness, worry: they all hurt. Don't hold to something that is hot, Saints. Anything that sears your mind is hot, it's a killer. It's a murderer, and it is illogical for Christians to hold on to something that's killing them. I don't understand why a person would hold on to fear. It is the most unreasonable, illogical thing. What would you think about someone who would go around just grabbing hot pieces of iron and holding on to them for five minutes and then lay them down? It is like you taking hold of fear with your mind and holding on to it all day long; Hold on to that hot anger for five minutes, and all day long you won't be worth much. All those thoughts will burn your mind more than hot iron would burn your hand. It's time that God's people quit letting the devil burn and sear their minds. It's my mind; he's not searing mine any more, his searing days are over. I examine things fast, according to the Word of God.

XI.   IT PREVENTS COUNTERFEITS OF FAITH.   Faith is in the heart. Romans 10:10 tells us that you, "CONFESS WITH YOUR MOUTH AND BELIEVE IN YOUR HEART." As your mind gets more and more renewed by the Word of God, you will get where you will not only know in your heart, but your mind will be able to tell the difference when you know it in your heart or know in your mind. The renewed mind will know the Word. The renewed mind will meditate the Scriptures. The renewed mind will have the Word of God in it, then the Holy Spirit can bring the Scriptures to your mind when you need them. Learn eight or ten Scriptures on **healing, prosperity, protection, guidance,** and **who you are in Christ, a conqueror and an overcomer.** (There are other areas you may desire to gather Scriptures on as well.) Begin to meditate upon them daily and it will revolutionize your life. You don't have to know a lot, just be disciplined and diligent enough to take those 50 verses and stay with them until you have renewed your mind with the Word of God. It is better to learn a little and do it, than to try to learn a lot and do nothing. Don't try to be learning too much too quickly. Realize that a basic foundation is required to move in faith in any area. Stay with the Word and it will grow inside of you. God loves you, you are God's children, and He desires you to know His Word. It's just a matter of being persistent and being diligent.

Isaiah 26:3, "THOU WILT KEEP HIM IN PERFECT PEACE, WHOSE MIND IS STAYED ON THEE: BECAUSE HE TRUSTETH IN THEE." The Word of God will help you keep your mind on the Lord.

XII. IT DEFEATS FEAR IN THE SOULISH REALM. Fear can't get into your heart because you are a new creature in Christ. II Corinthians 5:17 says, "THEREFORE IF ANY MANY BE IN CHRIST, HE IS A NEW CREATURE: OLD THINGS ARE PASSED AWAY; BEHOLD, ALL THINGS ARE BECOME NEW." We become new creatures in Christ. Fear doesn't come from God. You are born again, you are born of God, your spirit is a new creature in Christ. Your spirit is perfect; but your soul, your mind, your will, and your emotions, are not. As your mind is renewed, then you can defeat fear in the soulish realm. There is no fear in your spirit, so therefore any time fear comes it has to come to your mind. It comes through your feelings. You will see something, or feel something, and fear rises up inside of you. But when you know the Word of God and a fearful thought comes, you just automatically quote the Word of God. "THE ANGELS OF THE LORD ENCAMP ROUND ABOUT ME; NO EVIL SHALL BEFALL ME," and you go back to sleep. Or you wake up thinking about some problem that you're facing the next day, and you lie there fearful of what's going to happen the next day. You let that fear come into your mind. But praise God, "HE THAT IS IN YOU IS GREATER THAN HE THAT IS IN THE WORLD." When your mind is renewed by the Word of God, **fear can't take over.** You have authority over it. Fear always brings doubt; just quote the Word. I've learned in the years I've been walking with the Lord, that as I quote the Word I just have more and more confidence in that Word that it will do what it says it will do.

XIII. IT VOIDS THE LAW OF OLD ATTRACTIONS.

The mind, desires, lusts, etc.: you receive a new view on everything. A mind renewed by the Word of God voids the law of old attractions. It voids the law of fear, the law of distrust, the law of frustration, confusion, disappointment, discouragement, and disillusionment. Renewing the mind voids all of the old laws. Without a knowledge of the Word of God you don't have anything with which to cancel the old attractions. Here you are, saved and filled with the Holy Spirit, and the devil reminds you of something you did ten years ago and makes you feel bad, and puts you under condemnation. Renewing the mind voids all those old laws, old desires, dreams, aspirations. Not I but Christ lives in me. The law of grumbling and murmuring is voided by the law of rejoicing in the Lord always. The law of sadness is voided by the law of gladness. The law of prosperity voids the law of poverty. The law of health voids the law of sickness. The law of the new birth voids the law of hell for me; there's no way that I can go to hell; I am born again, born of God. I no more consider poverty and sickness than I do hell; I put them in the same qualification, they are not for me. I've been redeemed from them. They're voided out by the Name of Jesus, and by the Blood of Jesus. Hell is destroyed for me, there is no place in hell for me. Sickness is destroyed, there is no sickness for me. Poverty is destroyed, there is no place for poverty for me. I'm now in the law of God, the law of life, the law of the Spirit, the law of wisdom, the law of guidance. The old law of bad confessions is voided, only thinking on those things that are just, holy, pure and lovely, honest and of good report. A renewed mind voids the law of old attractions. When those old attractions get hold of you, you better mark it down. That means Satan still has a strong hold in your life, and your mind has not been renewed in that area. Christians, when you begin to serve the Lord, and you have troubles, it is not because you started doing new sins. It is because you do some of the old ones again. There's no new anger, it's that old anger; no new fear, it is that old fear; no new worry, it is that old worry; no new disappointment, it is that old disappointment. Saints, you don't live under that law any more. The old law of insecurity is voided with the law of confidence that He that is in you is greater that he that is in the world; that you can do all things through Jesus Christ. That old law of hate is gone, because the love of God is shed abroad in your heart. As the mind gets renewed the old things pass away. I can't think of any that I want to hold on to, but they still try to cling. They keep on trying to pull you back. You are a servant of the Lord Jesus Christ now. Saved, filled with the Holy Spirit, ordained by God to live the abundant, victorious life. Don't have any part of the other life. Make a proper judgment about it. Decide—God's way is the only way.

XIV. **ESTABLISHES A TEACHABLE MIND TO BIBLE CONCEPTS.** The more your mind is renewed by the Word of God gives you a better foundation to understand more. Any time you can't accept anything in the Bible, that proves your mind is not renewed in that area. It doesn't make any difference what you think, if it doesn't line up with the Word, you are wrong. But when your mind becomes renewed, it establishes a teachable mind and you begin to understand the Bible.

Everything you put your hand to will prosper. That's the Word of God. But an unrenewed mind says, Oh, I'm not sure about that. Mark 10:29-30 says whatever you give to the gospel, He will multiply it back one hundredfold now. If your mind is unrenewed, it is hard for you to believe that. You are not teachable in that area and can't really accept the Word of God as being the Truth. You know it says it, but yet you are unteachable there. Your old unrenewed mind rebels against that thought. Philippians 4:4 says rejoice in the Lord always. That old unrenewed mind says, it doesn't mean that. It says,

I don't have to do that. It argues with it, it debates with it. Any time your mind debates or argues with the Word of God, it indicates your mind is unrenewed in that area. Refuse to rebel against the Word, refuse to argue with the Word of God. "God, I don't know how You're going to do that; that's not my business. I'm just going to believe it because You said it." All your programming by the world will cause you to be unteachable about the spiritual things of God.

What did you think the first time you heard about Divine Healing? You hadn't been taught about it, so what did you do? Rebel. Unteachable. The more your mind is renewed, the more you can accept it. Living in victory every day, 365 days a year. The natural mind that's unrenewed says, Well now, that's kind of stretching it. John 16:13 says that the Holy Spirit, the Spirit of Truth, will guide me into all truth and show me things to come. I'm not going to get caught when things come. My mind is renewed by John 16:13. I confess John 16:13 every day: that the Holy Spirit, Spirit of Truth, guides me into all truth and He's showing me things to come. He's preparing me for the future. He's giving me revelation knowledge about the future from His written Word. Refuse to let your mind rebel against the Word of God. Many times I read the Scriptures and my mind wants to question them. Sometimes in the morning my body doesn't want to get up, but you know I don't let it do what it wants to do? I make it get up. Sometimes my mind reads the Word of God and doesn't want to believe it. If my mind does not accept the Word, it is wrong. It's been programmed by somebody else, because what's in my mind and what's in the Word doesn't line up, and it is because my mind is not right. The spirit man dominates my mind. The spirit man controls my life. The spirit man in me makes my mind and my body do the Word of God. My mind, my body, and my emotions sometimes don't want to do the Word. Renewal of the mind establishes a teachable mind.

XV. IT INCREASES THE POSSIBLITY OF PROSPERITY.
The more your mind is renewed by the Word of God, the more
you are going to prosper spiritually, and physically, and financially, and the more your relationship with God and with the
Holy Spirit, and even with brothers and sisters, will increase
because you will be able to walk diligently and faithfully
with the Lord Jesus Christ. Do you want to prosper? Here's
the key. Can a man prosper in engineering without a good
knowledge of engineering? No. Can a man prosper as a plumber, without a good knowledge in plumbing? No. The more
knowledge a man has about a field of endeavor (carpenter,
painter, plumber, doctor, lawyer, engineering, anything),
the more his knowledge the greater his prosperity. As your
mind is renewed by the Word of God, and the Holy Spirit
of God begins to control your life, you are going to live in
a land of prosperity that only Jesus Christ can bring you to,
a land of spiritual, physical, mental, and financial prosperity.
You will live in such a prosperous relationship with the Lord
Jesus Christ that you would rather spend time with Him than
anyone else in all the world. All the pleasures of the world and
the things of the world shall grow strange. I'm not talking about
pleasures that are wrong. There are a lot of pleasures in this
world that are good, clean pleasures for Christians; but even
they will begin to look strange in the presence of the Lord
Jesus Christ. You will become more sober minded than you've
ever been before, and then, Saints, He will begin to bless you
more in every area than you have ever been blessed before. That
is the promise of God for His children. That is the gospel.
That is what you call good news.

XVI. IT BIRTHS A STRONG ASSURANCE AND CON-
FIDENCE IN GOD AND HIS WORD. It causes a settling
down inside of you that nothing can shake. You simply say,
"I believe God." Until that mind begins to get renewed by the
Word of God, then you are unstable. Sometimes you will

have the assurance that the Word is true; next time you will say, "I'm not sure." When your mind gets renewed by the Word of God, the Holy Spirit will speak to you and you will begin to live in the land of confidence and assurance; confidence and assurance that God's Word is true; confidence and assurance that every bit of it is true; confidence and assurance that whatever God has said, He will do and He will perform. This is the confidence we have in Him: that He Who has begun a good work in us will finish it. Get confidence in healing, get assurance in prosperity, get assurance in the ability to live victoriously every day. A Holy Ghost assurance begins to rise up inside of you and it makes you to laugh at all the troubles of the world; at everything that comes your way, you just laugh, because you know that God's Word is true. He says when you go through the rivers and waters and fire, "I will be with you."

You are going to be just like the Hebrew children— you may be in the fire but there will be a fourth One there with you, and your hair shall not even be singed. You will be like Daniel in the lions' den. You will find yourself sometimes in the lions' den, but the lions can't devour you. You just walk around the lions of life. The lion of fear, the lion of frustration, the lion of confusion, the lion of disappointment, the lion of poverty, the lion of sickness: you just walk around among them. They roar and say you have to be sick, and you say, "Ha, Ha, shut your mouth." All those lions are roaring at you. They're saying, "We are mighty." You just say, "In the Name of Jesus, I walk in victory." When we get to know that Jesus is Lord of Lords and King of Kings, He's the Holy One, He's the Righteous One, He is the Almighty God, He's Saviour and Baptizer, Healer, Deliverer, Protector, Provider and King of Kings. God is so excited because we believe. It gives Him the opportunity to pour down all His blessings upon us.

OUTLINE ... CHAPTER FOUR
Methods of Conquest

I. KNOW YOUR RIGHT TO CONTROL YOUR MIND
II Corinthians 10:5, "Bringing into captivity every thought to the obedience of Christ."

II. KNOW ENEMY WILL RESIST GIVING UP TERRITORY HE HAS CONTROLLED FOR YEARS.

III. KNOW YOUR ENEMY'S TACTICS.

IV. KNOW JESUS DESTROYED SATAN'S POWER OVER US: I John 3:8, "For this purpose the Son of God was manifested, that he might destroy the works of the devil."
Control of mind for evil purposes.

V. KNOW YOU HAVE POWER OVER SATAN NOW:
Luke 10:19 "I give you power . . . over all the power of the enemy: and nothing shall by any means hurt you."
Satan-controlled mind can.

VI. KNOW THE WEAPONS YOU USE ARE NOT EARTH-LY: Ephesians 6:12, "We wrestle not against flesh and blood." II Corinthians 10:4, "The weapons of our warfare are not carnal."
God's Word in your mouth is your spiritual weapon.

VII. RENEWING YOUR MIND IS YOUR RESPONSIBILITY, NOT GOD'S: You change your thought pattern with Word food: Romans 12:1, "Ye present your bodies ... which is your reasonable service." Philippians 4:13; 4:19.

VIII. KNOW THE RENEWING OF YOUR MIND IS A PROGRESSIVE, NOT INSTANT, WORK:
Continuous effort. Diligent application.

IX. ESTABLISH AND MAINTAIN A CONFESSION OF YOUR RIGHTS, POSSESSION, POSITION, AND PURPOSE.

CHAPTER FOUR
Methods of Conquest

INTRODUCTION: It is God's will for you to have control of your mind. Your mind is as much yours as your hand, and you have a right to control your hand. Your mind is as much yours as your eyes, and you have the right to control your eyes. Many times you need to close them quickly because something may be coming toward them, or a sudden light that hits them. You need to realize that your mind is yours also, and glory to God, through the indwelling power of the Holy Spirit you can possess that territory. When Christians begin to possess their minds, by the Word of God, it brings them to a new dimension of walking with Jesus. The Bible tells us in Romans, chapter 12, verse 2: "BE NOT CONFORMED TO THIS WORLD; BUT BE YE TRANSFORMED BY THE RENEWING OF YOUR MIND . . ." The only way that you and I cannot be conformed to this world is when we have been transformed by the renewing of our mind by the Word of God. And if your mind is not renewed by the Word of God, the magnetic pull of the world, the drawing power of the world and what it stands for, will continually be pulling upon your unrenewed nature. It will continually be drawing you into traps. It will continually be causing you to fall and falter and fail, and do things that you know you should not do. The demonic power of the world will continue to hold you back and keep you from going to the heights that God has ordained for you. That pulling power of the world (unless your mind is renewed) will hinder you in living the abundant, victorious life that God has ordained for every believer to live.

If Jesus Himself would appear to us in the twentieth century, and you would ask Him, "Jesus, what should I think about?" what would be His answer? Philippians 4:8, the Word of God. Hebrews 13:8 says, Jesus Christ is the same yesterday, today and forever, so Jesus would point us to the unchanging Word of His Father. Malachi 3:6, "I AM THE LORD, I CHANGE NOT."

Since Jesus changes not, here is what He would tell you to think upon. "FINALLY, BROTHERS AND SISTERS, WHATSOEVER THINGS ARE **TRUE**, WHATSOEVER THINGS ARE **HONEST**, WHATSOEVER THINGS ARE **JUST**, WHATSOEVER THINGS ARE **PURE**, WHATSOEVER THINGS ARE **LOVELY**, WHATSOEVER THINGS ARE OF **GOOD REPORT**; IF THERE BE ANY **VIRTUE**, AND IF THERE BE ANY **PRAISE**, THINK ON THESE THINGS." (Philippians 4:8) This Scripture should be the guideline for your thought life. Any thought which hits your mind that doesn't line up with Philippians 4:8, ought to be immediately recognized and cast down (II Corinthians 10:5). Proverbs 6:2 says, "THOU ART SNARED WITH THE WORDS OF THY MOUTH, THOU ART TAKEN WITH THE WORDS OF THY MOUTH." When you begin to realize it is your mind, you can stop those thoughts because the Bible says, "SUBMIT YOURSELVES THEREFORE TO GOD. RESIST THE DEVIL, AND HE WILL FLEE FROM YOU." (James 4:7). You can stop those thoughts, you can cut them off. That doesn't mean that as you start you will begin to cut them off immediately. Sometimes you will battle for days and weeks. The truth of the matter is: it is easier to give in to them and blow your stack, ask God to forgive you, and then start over. Go ahead and yield to that anger, enjoy yourself telling them off; then when you get through, "Oh, 'God, I'm sorry." No, you're not. If you were, you wouldn't have done it; because you had the right to choose not to do it. Temporarily you lost control, but praise God, we want you to realize the methods of conquest, and come to a victorious walk with the Lord.

I.   YOU MUST KNOW YOUR RIGHT TO CONTROL YOUR MIND. II Corinthians 10:5, "BRINGING INTO CAPTIVITY EVERY THOUGHT TO THE OBEDIENCE OF CHRIST." What would be the obedience of God? Philippians 4:8 is one of them. Bringing every thought into the obedience of the Word of God. It says, "capture every thought." Every thought that hits your mind—capture it. This is how the devil deceives a lot of people. When you capture something, you take it under control. Take your mind and capture the thoughts that come, and if they line up with the Word of God then you eat them, digest them with your mind. If you put food in your mouth and it tastes real bad, what do you do? Go ahead and chew it up? No—you spit it out. If your hand touches something hot, you know what you have the right to do? Get it, away from it. Well, Saints, evil, bad thoughts are worse than your hand touching fire. They will sear and cause a blister on your mind. Your hand touches a hot fire and it will cause a blister that will bother you for a few days. You let your mind get on evil thoughts and it will cause a blister on your mind. It will bother you for a few days, won't it? It will condemn you. It will cause you hurt, or fear, or frustration, or insecurity or disappointment. But you need to realize and know your right to control your mind. Whose mind is this in your head? It is not the devil's. Should you not have the right to control your own possessions? Should you not have the right to control what your mind thinks on? You can't keep the devil from putting the thoughts there, because this is one of the rights he has because of the fall of Adam and Eve. But you have the power to chop them off. You have the power to stop them with the knowledge of the Word of God.

Philippians 4:13 says, "I CAN DO ALL THINGS THROUGH CHRIST WHICH STRENGTHENETH ME." Would that include my mind? Philippians 4:19 says, MY GOD SHALL SUPPLY ALL YOUR NEED." Believe you me, when you can't bring your mind under the control of the Word, you have a need, a big need. If you don't control it you live in fear. You live in fear, with insecurities, frustrations, disappointments, hurts and resentments. Know your right to control your mind. If you don't know this truth, you will never be able to bring it under control. The way your mind has been all of your life is that the devil has had free access to it, and you obeyed his commands.

II.   KNOW THE ENEMY WILL RESIST GIVING UP TERRITORY HE HAS CONTROLLED FOR YEARS. He's been a squatter, a poacher on your mind for so long, he thinks he owns it, and you believe he does, too. He has controlled your thoughts; he's put fear in your mind for so many years. He's put resentment, disappointment, hurt, depression, loneliness, envy, jealousy, freely in your mind for so many years. He's had free access to do it. When you start fighting him, he doesn't believe you. He says, "Now wait a minute, you've been afraid of that for twenty years. Next time you go back into a dark room you're going to be afraid again. I've trained you well for twenty years to be afraid." He says, "I've trained you to get angry every time somebody says that; you better do what I tell you." He's trained you every time winter comes, to "catch" a cold. And you better get one, because you've been trained that way. And you know what everybody gets—a cold. The enemy will resist giving up the territory he has controlled, when you begin to confess that your spirit controls your mind. When you begin to meditate in the Word of God, realize the devil is going to fight. Because he knows one of the keys to your maturity and one of your keys to your growth, and one of the keys to your receiving guidance and hearing from God, is for your mind to be controlled by the Holy Spirit of God. If your mind is controlled by the Holy Spirit of God, that means your mind is going to think in line with the Word. Then you have a Word mind, not a worldly mind. You have a mind that consistently thinks on the Word.

When I began to realize it was my mind, and the Word of God told me to think only on Philippians 4:8, I began to quote it every day. And I began to judge every thought that came to my mind by the Word of God. You can think right, but you are going to have to have something to judge and compare your thinking to. If a thought is good, just, holy, pure, lovely, honest and of good report, then I can think on it. I can remember sometimes I battled weeks on one thing. Somebody would say something to me that kind of stirred me up. Every time I'd see them the devil would remind me of what they said. After a few years I got to where someone could say something and I kept the victory. If you are always being reminded of what so and so said and what so and so did, or how so and so hurt you, that is not God. Those thoughts are coming from an impure and unholy, and unjust and evil source. You need to recognize it. When those thoughts hit your mind you need to recognize it doesn't line up with Philippians 4:8; therefore, since it does not line up with the Word of God, it can't be God. Pain hits your stomach, and you say, "By the stripes of Jesus I'm healed." What comes to an unrenewed mind? "Oh, maybe it is appendicitis. So and so had appendicitis and they died." That's an unrenewed mind. That's not thinking Bible, that's not good. Is that good, just, holy, pure, lovely, honest, and of good report? That's the opposite. Why think that way? I know why you think that way; you've been programmed that way. Realize that the enemy will always resist you. You're going to have to fight some battles. He has strongholds in every person's mind. There are some things in my mind that I fought some battles over. I didn't have to fight them only one time. He will counterattack, and counterattack, and counterattack. But if you stand on the Word, that mind will begin to live under the Blood of Jesus, and that mind will begin to live under the control of the Word of God and bring you into a new understanding of the Word ot God.

Do you know why most people can't bring their mind under the control of the Word? Laziness. It's easier just to let it go. Stop resisting the Word of God, and bring your mind under the control of the Word of God, and it will bring you into a new dimension in your walk with Jesus.

III. **KNOW YOUR ENEMY'S OPERATION TACTICS:** You need to know how he operates. He plants thoughts in your mind. Have you ever noticed how easy it is to remember what someone said bad about you? Have you ever noticed how those hurts have come back from yesterday? Those spirits of remembrance keep bombarding your mind with those things. This is one of his tactics. It is easy to recognize his tactics if you know Philippians 4:8. If a thought comes and it does not line up with Philippians 4:8, refuse that thought. You don't have to say it with your mouth, but the Bible says that's the best way to do it. Let the devil know. When I'm by myself that's what I do. A thought will come and I say, "That's not in line with Philippians 4:8; I refuse that thought in the Name of Jesus. Devil, I see you." Sometimes fifty times a day I've said, "Devil, I see you." The devil would say, "You sure sound stupid." All I'd say was, "I see you." I kept on doing it, I got to the place I could recognize him, quickly. You start by watching your thoughts and analyzing them with the Bible. Let's say you were saved when you were thirty years old. You have been thinking another way for thirty years. The devil has had control of you for thirty years. You think he's going to let you go overnight? You may be fifteen; he has had your mind that many years. He will always be trying to bombard you and bring the old failures back, bring the old frustrations back. If you don't believe me, go get your yearbooks out (when you went to high school). Look through them and see how many evil thoughts come back, what so and so did to you in the ninth grade; how mean that teacher was; I dated him for a while and he started dating somebody else. Oh, you will get some good ones. This is how the enemy operates.

IV. KNOW JESUS DESTROYED SATAN'S POWER OVER US: I John 3:8 says, "FOR THIS PURPOSE THE SON OF GOD WAS MANIFESTED, THAT HE MIGHT DESTROY THE WORKS OF THE DEVIL." He did it. He destroyed the works and gave you His authority and His power. Now He says, "You control it." Satan wants to control the minds of individuals for evil purposes. God wants to control their minds for holy purposes. When Satan controls the mind, what comes from it? Evil, fear, frustration, worry, discouragement, disappointment, hurt, insecurity, inferiority, stubbornness, resentment, hate, bitterness; all a sign of Satanic work. He wants to control your mind. He doesn't want your mind to be renewed by the Word of God. He knows the evil he's caused in this world by a mind controlled by him, and he knows a mind that is controlled by God is going to do great and glorious things for the Lord Jesus Christ. That's the will of God for you and me. "FOR THIS PURPOSE THE SON OF GOD WAS MANIFESTED, THAT HE MIGHT DESTROY THE WORKS OF THE DEVIL." I tell you what, Saints, if you don't resist him with the Word of God, you will live under this kind of garbage: "I'm so disappointed I can hardly go on." "It just hurt me so much." Sure it hurts, but I'll tell you what: I've come to realize this—it is very foolish if I let something hurt me when I can stop it. And Philippians 4:8 can stop those kinds of thoughts. If you don't entertain the thoughts they can't hurt. If you don't think how badly someone has mistreated you, it can't hurt you. It hurts because you meditate on it. It is better to keep thinking on Jesus.

When things come up now, all I can do is rejoice in the Lord. Last year I was up in Oakdale, Louisiana, visiting. My wife and some of her friends took the car and told me they would be back at 2:00 P.M. At 2:15 P.M. she wasn't back; 2:30 P.M. she was not back. At 2:45 P.M. they weren't back. About 3:15 she came driving up. About thirty minutes before that, it came to me all at once that I knew so much now about patience that I could not even get mad at her any more. I got tickled. I said, "I can't even jump on her. All I can do is rejoice in the Lord always." I was amazed; God had truly done a work in me! A lot of times it is that way as the Word of God begins to take over. Things will come up that should frustrate you, and you just look at them and say, "Glory to God." And people think you're crazy, because you are supposed to be like them. Something serious comes up when you should be worried, and you just say, "Hallelujah, Hallelujah, Glory, Hallelujah." People get mad at you because you don't worry like they do. If you really loved them you'd be doing like them, worrying. They don't realize that when they're worrying they can't believe God for anything. You begin to realize Satan's operation tactics and that he is going to resist you, but you can possess that territory by the authority of the Word of God.

V. KNOW THAT YOU HAVE POWER OVER SATAN NOW: Luke 10:19, Jesus says, "I GIVE YOU POWER. . . OVER ALL THE POWER OF THE ENEMY: AND NOTHING (Did He say a few things, or what did He say?) SHALL BY ANY MEANS HURT YOU." Saints, a Satan-controlled mind can hurt, a fear-controlled mind can hurt, a resentful mind can hurt. A mind that is controlled by bitterness or disappointment, or discouragement, or loneliness or heartache, or self-pity, can hurt. It will eat you up. But Jesus said, "I GIVE UNTO YOU POWER . . . OVER ALL THE POWER OF THE ENEMY: AND NOTHING SHALL BY ANY MEANS HURT YOU." It may look like it's going to hurt you. It may feel like it's going to hurt you. You may even think that it is going to hurt you. But if you hold to the Word of God, Saints, God will deliver you and bring you out of that situation. You must realize that you have power over Satan. How do you know that you have power? Because the Word of God says so. Jesus said He came to destroy the works of the devil. First John 4:4 says, "GREATER IS HE THAT IS IN YOU THAN HE THAT IS IN THE WORLD." Because II Corinthians 2:14 says He "ALWAYS CAUSETH US TO TRIUMPH IN CHRIST." "But I can't believe that." There's that unrenewed mind. What do you think about a mind that can't believe the Word of God? You know what they're saying? I think God lied. Christians do not realize how much trouble they cause themselves when they say, "I don't believe that." They don't realize they're calling God a liar. Jesus said He sent His Word and healed you. "I know He said it, but I believe He sent the doctors." Give me the chapter and verse. What you're saying is, "I think you lied, God; I like the doctors better; I have more confidence in the doctors; I'd rather use them than You." Those unrenewed minds rebel at that, they get mad. And you know who madness comes from? Guess! You know people will come to the service and hear the Word of God and manifest the devil by their reactions? Madness is not from God. He says, "I give you power over all the power of the enemy. I give you power over fear." Where does fear come from? Satan. Frustration, worry, self-pity, hurt, resentment, bitterness, disappointment, discouragement, depression? Jesus says He gave you power over all those things. Inside of you is the power of God over all things. You are going to have to start saying, "I've got power, power, over all the enemy." I started years ago quoting, "I've got power, power, power, power, power over all the enemy. Everything the devil does, I have power over him." The next day the temper would rise up. The devil would say, "You have power over what?" I'd say, "Father, forgive me in Jesus' Name. I've got power, power, power, over all the enemy." Four or five days later that temper would get away with me again, and the devil would say, "What did you say?" "I've got power, power, power, over all the enemy." I kept on confessing the Word of God. But now it is hard to get me angry. I'm going to go a little bit further, I'm going to say it's impossible. It's impossible by faith, and God is manifesting it. You begin to do it, and it will work for you just as it worked for me.

VI.   YOU MUST KNOW THE WEAPONS YOU USE ARE NOT EARTHLY. The weapons you're going to use to whip the devil and overcome him and bring your mind under control are not earthly. Ephesians 6:12 says, "WE WRESTLE NOT AGAINST FLESH AND BLOOD." The devil is the one who tries to take over your mind. He's not flesh and blood, so why should you think you can fight him with just your mind? You have a special weapon. II Corinthians 10:4, "THE WEAPONS OF OUR WARFARE ARE NOT CARNAL." That means fleshly, but it goes on to say, "BUT MIGHTY TO THE PULLING DOWN OF STRONGHOLDS." God's Word in your mouth and in your heart is your spiritual weapon. The Word of God is not from man so is not natural, carnal, or fleshly. How did Jesus defeat the devil the three times he came to Him? He said, "It is written." The devil wasn't a man, he was a spirit. Jesus fought him with a spiritual weapon, and yours is the same one, **The Word of God.** Luke 10:19 says He gave me power and authority over all the power of the enemy. As I confess that, it becomes my spiritual weapon. Philippians 4:13 says, "I CAN DO ALL THINGS THROUGH CHRIST WHO STRENGTHENETH ME." As I confess that, it becomes my spiritual weapon. Now if you are not using the Scriptures, how are you fighting the devil? What are you fighting him with? Flesh? The Scriptures say that we are not fighting against flesh and blood. The Word of God says that the weapons of our warfare are not carnal, so therefore, you must realize that the weapons that you use against the devil are not flesh and blood, not earthly; it is the Word of God. Put the Word of God in your mind and in your mouth and speak it, and decree it until God brings it to pass. If you're having a battle with fear, your weapon is II Timothy 1:7, "GOD HATH NOT GIVEN US THE SPIRIT OF FEAR; BUT OF POWER, AND OF LOVE, AND OF A SOUND MIND." You ought to be quoting II Timothy 1:7 while you're shaking in fear. When your heart gets to beating fast, you ought to be confessing, "God hasn't given me the spirit of fear, but of power, love, and of a sound mind." When the devil has knocked you down and you're running backward in defeat, you ought to be confessing, "I've got power over all the power of the enemy; I've got power over all the power of the enemy." While you're running backward vou ought to be shouting, "I've got power, I've got power, over all the power of the enemy." I've seen times when the devil has whipped me and knocked me down and he's on my chest, jumping. And I was saying, "I CAN DO ALL THINGS THROUGH CHRIST WHO STRENGTHENETH ME." Next thing I knew, I began to come up from there. Ever since then I've been on his chest. It is a lot better position. Recognize the weapon is not earthly, it is the Word of God. This is your weapon, this is what God has given unto you and me, to use to fight the devil and fight and defeat demons with. They come out in the **Name of Jesus,** they don't come out with the straining of the flesh. You are healed through the authority that is in the Name of Jesus, given to you by the Word of God.

VII. RENEWING YOUR MIND IS YOUR RESPONSI-
BILITY, NOT GOD'S. Study and meditate the Word of God.
You change your thought pattern with Word food. God is not
going to take this Word and just force feed it into your mind.
He says, you study and show yourself approved unto God
(II Timothy 2:15). You change your thought patterns, how?
Take Philippians 4:8 and say, "I'm only going to think on
things that are just, and holy, and pure, and lovely and honest
and of good report, virtuous and full of praise." The Word is
food. Romans 12:2 says, "YOU PRESENT YOUR BODIES
. . . WHICH IS YOUR REASONABLE SERVICE." Philippians 4:13 says, "I CAN DO ALL THINGS." Philippians
4:19 says, "MY GOD SHALL SUPPLY ALL MY NEEDS."
The only way you will come to the place where your mind is
under the control of the Word is when you recognize the renewing of your mind is your responsibility. He says, "BE
NOT CONFORMED TO THE THINGS OF THIS WORLD,
BUT BE YE TRANSFORMED BY THE RENEWING OF
YOUR MIND." He gives you what you need to renew it with,
the Word of God. He has given you the weapon, but you must
put it into action. God has given you the gun, but you have
to shoot it.

Joshua 1:8 says, Meditate his Word both day and night
and thy way shall be prosperous. Psalms 1:1-3 says meditate in
His Word both day and night, then it says you shall be like
a tree planted by the rivers and your leaves shall not wilt.
You will not get discouraged, you will not get frustrated,
you won't get disappointed. He says your leaves will not wilt,
and whatsoever you do shall prosper. Who is he talking to?
Those who meditate on His Word both day and night. It is
easy to let your mind meditate on something else. When you
wake up in the morning, what do you put your mind on?
If you don't make it think on the Word, I guarantee you it
will think on something else. You say, "Well, I just can't get
going." No wonder, with a mouth like that. "I'm just a sleepy
head." That's right, you are. "I just never have been able
to wake right up." That's right; you never will be able to,
either, with your mind thinking like that. "I'm just a slow

starter." That's right; you are and always will be. "If I don't get a full eight-hour sleep I can hardly get up." That's right, you can't. You're sluggish, and the spirit of sluggishness doesn't come from Jesus! You know what it is? You're lazy. You let your body control you for an hour, and after a while you finally get yourself under control. You try to make it get up and it says, "I'm not going to do it." It bosses you. The alarm clock goes off, and you go back to sleep. Renewing your mind is your responsibility. When you are awake your confession ought to be, "When I wake up I'm going to think on the things of God, and be diligent about it." Slothfulness and laziness are the greatest sins of Christians today. They permit the body to control, and the body becomes your god. It demands, and you can't control it. Realize that diligence is required if you are to renew your mind.

VIII.   RENEWING YOUR MIND IS A PROGRESSIVE, NOT AN INSTANT, WORK. The renewed mind says, "I'm going to fight until I win." The renewed mind says, "I won't stop until I win." It is not an instant work; it takes continuous effort, waking up in the morning and reaching for your Bible or Scripture confession cards. I've been doing it so long now, I would say that 99% of the time when I wake up my mind is thinking Scriptures. I can start meditating in the Word, and the next thing I know the Word begins to rise up inside of me and my body is strengthened and awake. I know where my source is, it is the Word of God. It is not instant, it requires diligent application. I'm like the Apostle Paul, I'm pressing "TOWARD THE MARK OF THE HIGH CALLING." I'm still pressing toward that mark. I'm getting more and more where things can come and I just keep on speaking the right thing, the Word of God. I'm getting where when a situation faces me and I should be getting angry and disturbed, I just keep speaking the Word of God because I know that the Word is true. He that is in me is greater than he that is in the world. "GOD IS NO RESPECTER OF PERSONS" (Acts 10:34). He said, "FIGHT THE GOOD FIGHT OF FAITH" (I Timothy

6:12). It's a fight. I know how it is to get up in the morning. As you renew your mind with the Word of God, you will get to the place where you don't want to go to bed too early and you don't want to sleep too late, because you don't want to be wasting that valuable time. You will come to realize all you need is seven hours of sleep.

Salvation is an instant work, but the renewal of the mind is a continual work. Suppose I fall? Ask God to forgive you, and get back with it again. What if I kind of slacked off the past few months, what do I do? Ask God to forgive you and get back with it. Keep staying with the Word of God, and next thing you know you'll be able to go longer and longer without failures. That is a good sign that your mind is being renewed.

IX. YOU MUST ESTABLISH AND MAINTAIN A CONFESSION OF YOUR RIGHTS AND POSSESSIONS AND POSITION AND PURPOSE. This means every day you must confess: "Praise God, the Holy Spirit, the Spirit of Truth, is my teacher and He's leading me and guiding me into all Truth. It is my mind; I have control of it. My mind functions in line with the Word of God, with Philippians 4:8. I only think on things that are just, pure, lovely, holy, honest and of a good report. I will not think on evil." The preceding are some that I confess. You ought to be saying this: "I will not think evil, I will not permit the devil to take my mind and cause fear, or frustration, or worry or confusion, or doubt. I will not permit my mind to go outside of the will of God. It's my mind, I have the right to possess it, I have the right to control it. God has said I can do all things through Jesus Christ who strengthens me. He says, delight yourselves in the Lord and He'll give you the desires of your heart. And the desire of my heart is for my mind to stay under the control of the Word of God." I don't want to be filled with all the fears, frustrations, and worries of yesterday, and I know you don't either.

I'm a child of God. Jesus has defeated the devil. I have

power over all the power of the enemy. My position is that of heir of God and joint heir with Jesus Christ. My position is that I'm seated in heavenly places with Christ Jesus. Glory to God, I have victory down here. I purpose in my heart that my mind is going to be renewed by the Word of God. My mind is going to be directed by Philippians 4:8. I refuse to let my mind be filled with garbage. I refuse to think evil of anybody or anything. I'm a murderer; I murder any thoughts that do not line up with the Word of God. Premeditated murder—I kill them. I purpose in my heart that I'm going to kill every thought that does not line up with the Word of God.

It is of great importance to establish and maintain your confession of your rights, possessions, position, and purpose as a child of the living God. Little children are a good example. Do you know what they do when they are learning how to walk? They skin their knees so many times, fall on their little noses, hurt their ears, get knots on their heads. They fall and cry and you pick them up and pet them and set them down on the floor, and they take off again. They'll run into something and cry, you will pick them up and tell them, "You're all right, honey," and they take off again. They won't stop until they can walk. They have that inbred in them. The Word of God has the same principle in you. If you fall, let Jesus pick you up and you go again. "I can do all things through Jesus Christ. I have power over all the power of the enemy." And you start right over again. You keep on confessing, "HE THAT IS IN ME IS GREATER THAN HE THAT IS IN THE WORLD."

Keep in mind the principles we have discussed in this chapter:

1.   Know your right to control your mind.
2.   Know the enemy will always resist.
3.   Know how the devil operates.
4.   Know Jesus destroyed Satan's power over the Christian.
5.   Know then that you have power over the enemy.

6. Know the weapon you use is the Word of God.
7. Know that renewing your mind is your responsibility.
8. Know that it takes time to reprogram your mind.
9. Know the importance of maintaining a confession of your rights, possessions, position in Christ Jesus.

OUTLINE ... CHAPTER FIVE
Advantages of Conquest

Romans 12:1-2

INTRODUCTION

I.   TEACHABLE: Romans 8:6, "To be spiritually minded is life and peace."
     Able to understand more so God is able to reveal more.

II. STRONG: Hebrews 12:3, "Lest ye be wearied, and faint in your minds."
     Word controlled minds endure.

III. SOUND: Romans 4:20, "Staggered not at the promise of God." James 1:8, "a double minded man is unstable in all his ways."

IV. DOER OF THE WORD: James 1:25, ". . . he being not a forgetful hearer, but a doer of the work, this man shall be blessed in his deed."

V.   DRAWS GOD'S LOVE AND REVELATION: John 14:21, "He that hath my commandments and keepeth them, he it is that loveth me: and he shall be loved of my Father, and I will manifest myself to him."

VI.   PEACE: Isaiah 26:3, "Thou wilt keep him in perfect peace, whose mind is stayed on thee: because he trusteth in thee."

VII.   SATAN'S KNOWLEDGE IS NOT EXALTED ABOVE GOD'S.

VIII.   NOT EASILY STOPPED IN FAITH'S OPERATION IN ANY AREA: Renewed mind an absolute for victory in any area.

CHAPTER FIVE
Advantages of Conquest
Romans 12:1-2

INTRODUCTION: In this chapter we are going to deal with the advantages of having your mind renewed by the Word of God. Your mind has to be controlled either by the word of the world or the Word of God. It is either controlled by fear or faith, worry or peace, gladness or madness. As believers in the Lord Jesus Christ, having been filled with the Holy Spirit, we have been called of God to live an abundant, victorious, overcoming life. It is time we begin to move forward as we never have before, that our minds be controlled by the Holy Spirit of the living God.

Romans 12:1-2, "I BESEECH YOU THEREFORE, BRETHREN, (I challenge you)·BY THE MERCIES OF GOD, THAT YE PRESENT YOUR BODIES A LIVING SACRIFICE (when the sacrifice was dead someone else put it upon the altar; you and I are living sacrifices; we are supposed to put ourselves upon the altar as a living sacrifice), HOLY, ACCEPTABLE UNTO GOD, WHICH IS (a normal thing for you to do) YOUR REASONABLE SERVICE." You mean that's just a reasonable thing? That's right. It is reasonable and sensible for you to have your mind conformed to the Word of God. It is reasonable and sensible for you to live in victory every day. It is just as unreasonable and unsensible for a Christian to be defeated. For an individual who doesn't know God, it is a reasonable thing for him to live a defeated life. It is a reasonable thing for a lost man to worry. It is unreasonable for a Christian to worry. Jesus said five times, don't worry ("Take no thought," Matthew 6).

It is reasonable for a lost man to be sick. But it is unreasonable for a Christian to be sick when he has the healing power of God available (Isaiah 53:4,5; I Peter 2:24). It is a reasonable service to present yourself as a living sacrifice.

Romans 12:2, "AND BE NOT CONFORMED TO THIS WORLD (don't be adjusted and adapted to this world): BUT BE YE TRANSFORMED BY THE RENEWING OF YOUR MIND, THAT YE MAY PROVE WHAT IS THAT GOOD, AND ACCEPTABLE, AND PERFECT, WILL OF GOD." If you desire to prove what is the good, and acceptable, and perfect, will of God, the only way you can is by **not being conformed to the world and being transformed by the renewing of your mind.** Until you and I recognize the value of having our minds renewed and begin to do it (by studying and by the exercise of our faith), then we are never going to prove what is the good, and acceptable, and perfect will of God. Purpose in your heart to prove it. "FOR I SAY, THROUGH THE GRACE GIVEN UNTO ME, TO EVERY MAN THAT IS AMONG YOU, NOT TO THINK OF HIMSELF MORE HIGHLY THAN HE OUGHT TO THINK: BUT TO THINK SOBERLY, ACCORDING AS GOD HATH DEALT TO EVERY MAN (not just a few) THE MEASURE OF FAITH." (Romans 12:3) With that measure of faith you can believe in God, exercise your faith and bring your mind under the control of the Holy Spirit of God.

Let's observe some of the advantages of having your mind under the control of the Holy Spirit.

I.   YOU BECOME TEACHABLE. Romans 8:6 says, "TO BE SPIRITUALLY MINDED IS LIFE AND PEACE." The first part of that verse says that to be carnally minded, and fleshly minded, or sense minded,or naturally minded, or worldly minded is death. As long as I was worldly minded I was sick. As long as I was logical, and reasonable, and earthly minded, carnally minded, fleshly minded and worldly minded — I worried. Because that is the natural, normal, worldly, earthly, sensible, carnal thing to do. But it is not the spiritual thing to do. Today, most people are not teachable about worry. And Jesus said five times, don't worry (take no thought). Being teachable is being able to understand more; therefore, God is able to reveal more. One of the advantages of having your mind renewed by the Word of God is that you will begin to believe things you couldn't believe before. I couldn't believe in Divine Healing before. All I could believe in was medical healing. I was not teachable at all about Divine Healing. I knew God was able, I knew God **could** do it, but I didn't know if God **would** do it. As my mind began to be renewed by the Word of God, and as I began to meditate the Scriptures on Divine Healing, I became teachable. Do you know what I received? Healing. Now I walk in health because I became teachable according to the Word of God. I'm very unteachable as far as the world is concerned. I don't want to know any more of their junk. It kept me worried, sick, in debt, frustrated, confused, and disturbed. To be spiritually minded is life and peace. You can't have life and peace and worry at the same time. When the mind gets renewed by the Word of God you come into a new plateau of understanding and grasping and comprehending the spiritual truths of God, and become **other world minded** instead of **this world minded.** You begin to rebel against the teachings of this world because you begin to realize they do not come from God. You become teachable to the Holy Spirit of God, but unteachable as far as man is concerned. When you become teachable toward God, people will call you crazy.

I have people tell me all the time that it is ridiculous to think that you can live without worry. Now can you imagine a Christian thinking that it is ridiculous to even think you can live without worry, and yet Jesus said five times, don't worry? When your mind begins to be renewed it will be more teachable than it has ever been before. You couldn't teach me concerning praising God. I was unteachable. I was reverent, and dead. If a shout would build up inside of me I couldn't let it out for anything in the world. When I became teachable about praise and worshipping the Lord, it brought life and peace to my inner man. When you become teachable, God will teach you some things that most people can't be taught.

You know what the people of Jesus' day thought about Him? They thought He was crazy. They thought that He had lost His mind. Even His mother and His brothers thought He was beside Himself. He was! He was teaching the things of God. And whenever ministers today teach the things of God, people are going to think they are beside themselves. You don't need to be taught any more the ways of man. We've been taught that since we were born. It is time, through the renewal of the mind, we understand the ways of God, and move and live in the ways of God, to prepare for the return of the Lord Jesus Christ. Being teachable is being meek. Teachable means yieldedness; that means you will yield to the Word. One of the keys to being used by God and being blessed of God is being teachable.

II. STRONG. Hebrews 12:3 says, "LEST YE BE WEARIED, AND FAINT IN YOUR MINDS." A Word controlled mind endures. As your mind is renewed by the Word of God, and you plant the Word of God in your mind, you won't be weary and faint in your mind. This is how the devil defeats 99% of Christians. You read the Word, and believe it and you desire to do it, and you begin doing it. But the devil starts bombarding your mind, and your senses, and puts so much pressure on your mind that you get weary. One of the advantages of the conquest of the mind is that your mind becomes strong with the Word of God, and you become yielded to the Holy Spirit of God. The devil can bombard you from a hundred different directions, but he can't get to your mind, because Isaiah 26:3 says, "THOU WILT KEEP HIM IN PERFECT PEACE, WHOSE MIND IS STAYED ON THEE: BECAUSE HE TRUSTETH IN THEE." If the mind is not renewed it will become weary. The devil knows how to bring enough pressure against you spiritually, physically, mentally, and financially to whip you every time. But when your mind is renewed by the Word of God you can hold to the Word of God. A Word controlled mind endures. Once a man's mind is renewed, the devil can't make it turn loose. His body is saying, "I'm dying," and his mind is saying, "I'm healed." His bank account says, "You will never make it," but his mind renewed by the Word of God says, "I have plenty." It is important for you to have your mind renewed if you intend to be strong in the Lord. Until it is renewed, and the more it is renewed, then the stronger you will be, because you will be able to hold fast to the Word of God.

III.   SOUND.   Romans 4:20 says, "ABRAHAM STAGGERED NOT AT THE PROMISE OF GOD." What had God promised him? He said, "I'm going to give you a son, and I'm going to make you the father of many nations." God said, "The people that will come forth from you will be like the stars in heaven." It takes a sound mind renewed by the Word of God to receive the promises of God; like — don't worry, don't be afraid, don't fear anything. It takes a mind renewed by the Word of God to hold on to the positive promises of God.

James   1:8 says, "A DOUBLE MINDED MAN IS UN-STABLE IN ALL HIS WAYS." As long as you are double minded you are unstable in all your ways. You will never be able to hold on to the Word. A double minded man, a two-faced man, two-souled man, a man that one time says he's going all the way and the next time he doesn't know where he's going: he's double minded, therefore he is unstable. Make up your mind to one thing — I am going to be faithful. When you make up your mind to be faithful, next thing you know your mind is getting renewed and you start receiving some of the good things that you haven't been receiving. Some people are faithful as long as they are receiving. When they don't get what they believed for and prayed for, they become unfaithful. That is an indication that they had a root of unfaithfulness to start with. They were faithful based upon the hope of what they were going to receive.   Make up your mind to become faithful — rain, shine, sleet or snow, up or down, under or on top, above or beneath; "I'm going to be faithful to the Lord Jesus Christ." God's Word is true, because God is true. Keep your mind upon God. Satan brings so much pressure against your mind until your mind gets off of God and on your problem. It gets off the Word and onto the possibilities, or the suppositions, or what if's. Philippians 4:13 says, "I CAN DO ALL THINGS." Remember, it doesn't come immediately, it comes progressively, a step at a time. How do you swim across a lake? A stroke at a time. How do you get in your car, one leap or a step at a time?

You know how you get your mind renewed? A step at a time, one Scripture at a time. As you are growing, your mind is being renewed.

IV. DOER OF THE WORD. What is the opposite from a doer? A hearer! James 1:25 says, "BEING NOT A FORGETFUL HEARER, BUT A DOER OF THE WORK, THIS MAN SHALL BE BLESSED IN HIS DEED." Who shall be blessed, the hearer or the doer? You can hear and hear and hear, but you will never be blessed in your deed. God says He only blesses the doers. You know how to become blessed out of praising God? Begin to do it. I became a doer in the giving, sowing money; you know what happened? When I got out of the hearing business and got into the doing business, I became blessed in my deed. What deed? In my giving deed. In my praising deed. Saints, I spoke in tongues for weeks and weeks and didn't get blessed. I didn't feel anything. When I was baptized in the Holy Spirit I didn't have any emotional experience at all. And the devil battled me. He said, "What do you feel?" And I said, "Nothing!" I simply found in I Corinthians 14:4 that it says speaking in tongues edifies, and I knew that I could not be a hearer, I had to be a doer, if I was going to be edified. So by the act of my will I started speaking in tongues every day, for hours. I became a doer of the Word. My mind became renewed by the Word that speaking in tongues edifies. He says speaking in tongues will edify you, speaking in tongues will charge you up. I became a doer of the Word. It was many days later that I actually felt the abiding presence of the Holy Spirit of God. The Word says, "BE NOT A FORGETFUL HEARER." l was not a forgetful hearer. The Word says speaking in tongues edifies you. "THIS MAN SHALL (mandatory) BE BLESSED IN HIS DEED." Praise God, we were blessed in our deed, we were blessed in our giving and God began to multiply it back. We do it God's way and He takes care of us." "GIVE, AND IT SHALL BE GIVEN UNTO YOU; GOOD MEASURE, PRESSED DOWN AND SHAKEN TOGETHER, AND RUNNING OVER." (Luke 6:38) The world says you have to give where you can see a return. That is not faith. Faith gives it unto the Lord and looks to God for the return.

V.   DRAWS GOD'S LOVE AND REVELATION. John 14:21 says, "HE THAT HATH MY COMMANDMENTS AND KEEP-ETH THEM," (is that renewing your mind?). If your mind is renewed by the Word you have His commandments, you have His Word, then you will be able to keep them. "HE IT IS THAT LOVETH ME: AND . . .SHALL BE LOVED OF MY FATHER, AND I . . . WILL MANIFEST MYSELF TO HIM." This one Scripture makes it worth it for you to study and get your mind renewed. Learn the Word, get your mind renewed by His commandments, His precepts, His Word. You have the Word in your mind and in your heart. All of the Christians who tell you they love God, if they don't have the Word and they don't keep the Word, they are not loving Him. They are saying it with their mouths but the only way they can prove it is by having the Word and keeping it. They can tell me all day long that they love God. He says, "HE THAT HATH MY COM-MANDMENTS AND KEEPETH THEM, HE IT IS THAT LOV-ETH ME: AND SHALL BE LOVED OF MY FATHER AND I WILL MANIFEST MYSELF TO HIM." That's us. This is why we are getting our minds renewed, so that we can have His commandments and keep His commandments. That will be the proof of our love. Love always demonstrates itself by ac-tion. Love for God will demonstrate by action, by having His commandments, studying and meditating them and then keeping them. That is how you prove you love Him. Get your mind renewed by the Word of God, be teachable, obey His Word, be strong, be sound in the Lord, and then you will draw His love. "AND SHALL BE LOVED OF MY FATHER"; this is Jesus speaking. He says on top of that, "My Father is going to love you." That's good, but Jesus says, "I will reveal myself to you." He says, "I'm going to unfold the Word to you. I'll speak to you, I'll lead you, and I'll guide you." That is a definite ad-vantage to having your mind renewed by the Word of God. "He (you and I) IT IS THAT LOVETH ME." If I tell my wife

109

I love her, don't you think I need to show her? Many Christians say I love God, I love God, I love God; but they don't have His Word and they don't keep it. You know what they are? They are liars, just like I'd be if I didn't express my love to my wife. Love is always followed by an action. Love is something that is demonstrated.

VI.   PEACE. Isaiah 26:3 says, "THOU WILT KEEP HIM IN PERFECT PEACE, WHOSE MIND IS STAYED ON THEE: BECAUSE HE TRUSTETH IN THEE." Who is going to have the peace? The mind that is stayed on God. Until it gets renewed you can't keep it fixed. He whose mind is fixed upon Jesus will have perfect peace "BECAUSE HE TRUSTETH IN THEE." You can't really keep your mind stayed on God unless you trust in Him. If you trust in something else — that's what your mind will be stayed upon. This is why this mind has to be renewed, because when it is renewed you can come into peace. Jesus says, five times, do not worry (Matthew, chapter 6). Philippians 4:4 says, "REJOICE IN THE LORD ALWAYS." The only way you can be at peace with God over that Scripture is to do it. Be ye not a hearer but be ye a doer of that Word. "THOU WILT KEEP HIM IN **PERFECT PEACE**." I've held to that Scripture many times. I would say, "My mind is fixed upon God and God's Word because I trust in Him." As your mind gets more renewed you are going to receive more miracles.

VII.   SATAN'S KNOWLEDGE IS NOT EXALTED ABOVE GOD'S. Satan's knowledge says, Fear! God's knowledge says, "GOD HATH NOT GIVEN YOU THE SPIRIT OF FEAR, BUT OF POWER, AND OF LOVE, AND OF A SOUND MIND." When your mind is renewed, Satan's knowledge is not exalted above God's knowledge. By this I mean Satan's knowledge does not control your mind and bring you under his control. Your mind stays under the control of the Word of God and the Holy Spirit of God. Whenever Satan has a hold upon your life and is controlling your life by anger, fear, frustration, resentment, bitterness, disappointment, or whatever it might be, whenever that knowledge is exalted above the knowledge you know about

110

God, Satan is exalted in his word above God's Word in your life at that particular moment. The Word of God must be exalted. Jesus says if He be lifted up He will draw men to Himself. As His Word is first place in our lives, we can walk in the anointing of the Spirit of God and walk in the abundance and the victory that natural men have never known, and we can walk in the abundance and victory that most Christians have never known and will never know. It is available for them. We are learning things now that have always been available; we are not learning things that are new. They have always been available; we just didn't know anything about them. God is pulling the blinders from our eyes and the Holy Spirit is working in our lives to bring us to receive the truths of God, that we might walk in the totality of the victory that God has ordained before the foundation of the world for His people. We are in the last days, and when sin abounds, grace shall superabound. Things are getting bad in this world; that means that God's grace is going to superabound. The more we see that sin is on every hand today, we know then that the coming of our Lord and Saviour, Jesus Christ, is near. The last is going to be much greater than the first. That means we're coming closer and closer to a mighty anointing of the Spirit of God. That means we're coming closer and closer to the fulfillment of John 14:12 where it says, "VERILY, VERILY, I SAY UNTO YOU, HE THAT BE-LIEVETH ON ME, THE WORKS THAT I DO SHALL HE DO ALSO; AND GREATER WORKS THAN THESE SHALL HE DO; BECAUSE I GO UNTO MY FATHER."

You can hardly watch TV; even the good programs are loaded with junk. Well, all the heathen know is junk, they can't do anything else. I don't like it, I'm against it; but I've already read the last page, and it says ¬ "We win." I know what's going on, the wicked one is manifesting himself in a greater way today. He's getting bolder — Satan worshippers. When Jesus died He said it was "FINISHED." Satan's days are numbered. He's already been found guilty; he's already been judged; all we are waiting for is hanging time. I know it is getting bad in the world, but as he manifests himself (the Bible talks about this), it says we're going to know the season and the times because we will begin to see him manifest himself. There is no reason to be afraid. It means that it is getting closer to the rap-up, closer to a mighty manifestation, closer to more people getting saved than ever before. It may look like we're losing; it may look like we are on the short end of the stick, but we're not. We are the children of the King. The victory is ours — signed, sealed and delivered. In these last days as Satan begins to manifest his power, God is going to manifest His power. God is going to give us understanding and revelation of the Word of God like man has never known. God is raising up a great end time army, and millions are going to be saved and filled, and healed and delivered. God's glory is going to be shown on the earth and manifested right in the midst of the wickedness. He says, "I will prepare a table for you in the presence of your enemy." Right in Satan's face, right in the midst of gross sin, God is preparing a banquet table and people are going to come from the north, the south, the east, and the west, and they are going to partake of Jesus and be saved. There is nothing to be afraid of, nothing to be fearful about; Jesus is Lord of all. He is still ruling and reigning. Just something to shout about.

When Jesus died, Satan thought he won. Oh, but death couldn't keep Him; and the devil can't keep God's people down in the last days. I'm looking forward to being a part of God's end time army. I'm going to learn things like I've never learned before. When that power really begins to manifest, it is going to be the time for the greatest anointing for God's people. Satan's knowledge is not exalted above God's. Jesus is King of kings and Lord of lords. He is the Almighty God. Satan is already judged. He has a place prepared for him. He's on the death row, the sentence is final. All up and down this country people are beginning to get saved. By great numbers they are going to come to know Jesus.

VIII. NOT EASILY STOPPED IN FAITH'S OPERATION IN ANY AREA. A mind that has been renewed can hold to the Word of God, and is not easily stopped in faith operation in any area: spiritual, physical, mental, or financial. When a mind is renewed by the Word of God and knows how to hold to the

Word of God, it can't be stopped. Romans 8:37 says you and I are "MORE THAN CONQUERORS" through Christ Jesus. Philippians 4:13 says that "I CAN DO ALL THINGS THROUGH CHRIST WHICH STRENGTHENETH ME." I John 4:4 says, "GREATER IS HE THAT IS IN YOU THAN HE THAT IS IN THE WORLD." John 15 says that Jesus is the Vine and we are the branches. He says without Him we can do nothing, but we are not without Him. We are grafted into God, into union with Jesus Christ, and the Holy Spirit of God dwells inside of us. As a branch draws what it needs from the vine, you and I, because we are connected to God, draw from God that which we need to live abundant, victorious lives, to testify of the greatness and the glory of God. Not by might and not by strength but by the Spirit of the living God. I cannot produce any spiritual results by myself, but because I'm connected to Jesus; He is the Vine and I'm the branch. I can draw everything that I need from Him, everything that I need to live the abundant, victorious life, to be a testimony to witness for Jesus Christ. You are branches and Jesus is the Vine, and you have been grafted into that eternal Truth; grafted into union with the Father God, the Son, and Holy Spirit. Everything that is in the vine can come forth into the branch. His love, His joy, His peace, His faith, His anointing: it is yours and it is mine because we are in union with Jesus Christ, the Son of the living God. Born of flesh I received arms,. legs. eyes, nose and mouth: attributes for me to use to live in this world. But because I've been born of God, I received the God kind of attributes to be a testimony and witness to Jesus Christ, the Son of God. As our minds become renewed more and more by the Word of God, we will come to a greater understanding of the revelation of God. We will begin to see the things of God more clearly than we ever have before. The blinders shall fall from our eyes, and the Word of God shall come alive like it never has before. Your heart, your spirit, your inner man, shall shout and rejoice. The Spirit of God rising up inside of God's people, evangelizing this world, preaching Jesus, teaching Jesus, healing the sick, casting out devils, operating in all the gifts and manifesting all the fruits, that

113

Jesus might be glorified; that the King of kings might be magnified, that the Name of Jesus shall be spoken on many more lips.

It is good to be a Christian, and it is good to know that God's Word is true.

Remember, there are definite advantages to renewing your mind with the Word of God; you become teachable, you become strong, sound in God's Word; you become a doer of the Word, and not a hearer only. You draw God's love to you and then revelation of the Word begins to enter your heart. You have peace — perfect peace — because the Prince of Peace controls your life. As your mind is conquered and renewed, a realization that Satan's knowledge is never exalted above God's comes to your understanding. Remember that as your mind is renewed, you begin to walk in victory in that area. God's will and purpose is total victory in every area of the believer's life.

OUTLINE ... CHAPTER SIX
Words of Wisdom in Conquest

INTRODUCTION.

I.   **PROPER CONCEPT:** Proverbs 23:7, "For as he thinketh in his heart, so is he." Never contradicts Word.

II.   **DELIVERANCE:** II Peter 2:9, "The Lord knoweth how to deliver the godly out of temptations."

III. **ANSWERS:** Proverbs 15:1, "A soft answer turneth away wrath: but grievous words stir up anger."
       Pride and passion — Both will demand.

IV.   **CONTENTION:** Proverbs 13:10, "Only by pride cometh contention."

V.   **PRIDE:** Proverbs 16:18, "Pride goeth before destruction, and an haughty spirit before a fall." Climber.

VI.   **HUMILITY:** Proverbs 15:33, "Before honour is humility." Preserving grace - I Peter 5:6, "Humble yourselves under the mighty hand of God, that he may exalt you in due time."

VII. **OFFENSIVE:** Proverbs 18:19, "A brother offended is harder to be won than a strong city: and their contentions are like the bars of a castle."

VIII. **STABILITY:** Proverbs 16:3, "Commit thy works unto the Lord, and thy thoughts shall be established."

IX. **PERCEPTION:** Proverbs 16:2, "All the ways of a man are clean in his own eyes."

X. **SNARE:** Proverbs 29:25, "The fear of man bringeth a snare."

XI. **FLATTERY:** Proverbs 28:23, "He that rebuketh a man afterwards shall find more favour than he that flattereth with the tongue."

XII. **PROMOTION:** Psalm 75:6-7, "Promotion cometh neither from the east, nor from the west, nor from the south. But God is the judge: he putteth down one, and setteth up another."

XIII. **KNOWLEDGE:** I Corinthians 8:1, "Knowledge puffeth up, but love edifieth."

XIV. **TALKING:** Proverbs 10:19, "In the multitude of words there wanteth not sin: but he that refraineth his lips is wise."

XV. **USEABLE:** Mt. 20:26-28, "But whosoever will be great among you, let him be your minister; and whosoever will be chief among you, let him be your servant; even as the son of man came not to be ministered unto, but to minister, and to give his life a ransom for many."

XVI. **FUTILITY OF HUMAN EFFORT TO PRODUCE ANY SPIRITUAL RESULTS.**

CHAPTER SIX
Words of Wisdom in Conquest

INTRODUCTION: The subject in this chapter requires insight into various truths. The Bible is the Word of Wisdom. It is the mind of God. When you receive a word of wisdom from God or a Scripture from God, and you begin to follow it, it becomes guidance for your life. So you hear from God, you get a word from Him, a Scripture directly from Him; it becomes guidance for your life. What you could call this is some words of guidance, some various truths that will enable you to walk straight as you begin to take control of your mind. Most of these are from Proverbs, just little words of wisdom, words of truths that most people overlook.

I.   **PROPER CONCEPT.** Proverbs 23:7 says, "FOR AS HE THINKETH IN HIS HEART, SO IS HE." The heart that is renewed by the Word of God never contradicts the Word. Your mind will contradict the Word, but the heart, the inner man, the spirit, will never contradict the Word of God. It doesn't say "as the man thinketh in his mind, so is he." It says, "AS HE THINKETH IN HIS HEART, SO IS HE." If you are going to come into the place where your mind is under the control of the Word of God, and led by the Spirit, directed by the Word of God, then you are going to have to realize that it is not how you think in your head; it is as you think in your heart. And any time your head starts to contradict your heart, go by your heart. Any time any knowledge in your mind contradicts the Word of God, refuse it. The spirit man in you is that new creature in Christ, and will never go contrary to the Word of God. The Holy Spirit lives inside of you, you are born again, born of God; the same Spirit that raised Christ from the dead dwells in you. That Spirit in you will never contradict the Word, because it is the Spirit of God.

As you begin to walk with God and believe for your mind to be renewed, realize you must never contradict the Word of God. Many times your mind will think contrary to the Word of God. You will be believing God for a healing, and receive it. But your mind starts telling you something else: Feel that pain. Look at the way the situation is; you'll never make it. The money will never come in. You will never get healed of that cancer. The family problem will never be straightened up. When your mind tells you things that do not line up with the Word of God, it is contradicting the Word of God, so reject those thoughts. Say, "As I think in my heart, as I think in my spirit, that's what I'm going to go by. I'm going to go by the Word of God."

II. DELIVERANCE. II Peter 2:9, "THE LORD KNOWETH HOW TO DELIVER THE GODLY OUT OF TEMPTATIONS." While you are learning to bring your mind under the control of the Word of God you are going to have to realize that many temptations will come your way. The devil will try to come and defeat you. He's going to try to lead you astray. He's going to try to lead you to contradict the Word of God. He's going to try to lead you to question the Word of God. He's going to try to lead you to say, how can God do it? or why hasn't God already done it? What you need to realize is that "THE LORD KNOWETH HOW TO DELIVER THE GODLY OUT OF TEMPTATIONS." He knows how to deliver you and me out of every temptation that comes our way. Praise God, the temptation to think wrongly, the temptation to say, "Well, I don't believe my mind will ever get renewed by the Word of God. I just can't believe that I will ever be able to think good, pure, holy, thoughts as Philippians 4:8 says." When that temptation comes, God can deliver you out of it, for you to believe the Word of God that says only think on those things that are just, holy, pure, lovely, honest, and of good report. I praise God that as we study the Word of God we can be assured in our minds and our hearts that God is able to deliver us out of every temptation.

III. **YOUR ANSWERS:** Proverbs 15:1 says, "A SOFT ANSWER TURNETH AWAY WRATH: BUT GRIEVOUS WORDS STIR UP ANGER." The general meaning of this is that, for example, if a bull is running at you, you let it go by. If someone gets angry at you, put a soft answer back at them, because if you don't put back a soft answer you're going to put back a hard answer. Why do you put back a hard answer? Pride. Then what happens to your temper? It begins to flair up so pride and passion come into play, you see, and it takes two people. If you want to keep yourself out of a lot of trouble, learn that a soft answer turns away wrath. I've seen many times that I should have given a soft answer, and if I had, it wouldn't have been a heated argument. I've seen times when it did happen, I just gave a soft answer, I didn't argue with them. I didn't debate with them, and you know what it did. Like pouring water on their anger. The fire will go out a lot quicker. When somebody is angry and you hit them with some words, those hard words are like wood on the fire. They say something to you, then you say something back to them; they say something back at you, and you say something back to them. If you don't watch this you will never bring your mind under the control of the Word of God, because the devil is going to always have someone around jabbing you. You must learn to give soft answers.

IV. **CONTENTION:** How does contention come? Only by pride. When you're in contention with somebody, you know what it is? You will never bring your mind under the control of the Word of God if that pride is not dealt with. The Word of God says, "ONLY BY PRIDE COMETH CONTENTION." (Proverbs 13:10) You know what makes you fight back? Pride, defending my rights. You are supposed to be dead.

Maybe some neighbor says something about you, it may not be the truth, but you really want to defend yourself. What you're saying is, "If it was the truth it wouldn't be so bad; it is a lie, so I have to straighten that up." You know what that is? Pride. Only by pride comes contention. When there is contention between you and another brother, you and another sister, between husbands and wives, you know what's there. Somebody is demanding their rights. If you don't give it to them, they are mad. Every time contention comes up, the Lord says, only by pride comes contention, so realize this and renew your mind in this area.

V. **PRIDE:** Proverbs 16:18, "PRIDE GOETH BEFORE DESTRUCTION, AND AN HAUGHTY SPIRIT BEFORE A FALL." A person with a haughty spirit is prideful; they are climbers. They always want to win, they want to win every argument, they want to get the last word in. If your mind is going to come under the conquest of the Word of God, you can't move in pride, because pride goeth before a fall. It opens the door for defeat. When you have a prideful spirit, a haughty spirit, thinking that you are better than other people, you are in for a fall. With those kinds of things in your life, Saints, you will never be able to get your mind renewed by the Word of God. You will have a haughty spirit, and therefore be filled with pride. You will always be having contentions. You will not be giving soft answers, but a hard word. They will give a hard word, and you will give a hard word; they strike you, and you strike them. But God says give soft answers and you'll stay out of contention.

VI. **HUMILITY:** Proverbs 15:33 says, "BEFORE HONOUR IS HUMILITY." For God to honor you is humility. Men may give you honor, but it is not the real thing. Humility is the preserving grace of God. I Peter 5:6, "HUMBLE YOURSELVES UNDER THE MIGHTY HAND OF GOD, THAT HE MAY EXALT YOU IN DUE TIME." Pride will keep a person from being humble. Before honor is humility. What is being humble? The basic Greek says it means, "a low, low feeling."

120

The word "humble" means to estimate yourself correctly. If you estimate yourself correctly, that means you must have some basis to estimate yourself. You can estimate yourself by what people think about you, but you don't want to do that. You can estimate yourself by what you think about yourself, but you don't want to do that. There is just one way to estimate yourself and judge yourself the right way, according to the Word of God. The humble man is a man who judges himself as the Word of God judges. "I CAN DO ALL THINGS THROUGH CHRIST WHO STRENGTH- ENETH ME"; that's humility. I judge myself as God judges: "NOT I LIVE, BUT CHRIST LIVETH IN ME"; "HE THAT IS IN ME IS GREATER THAN HE THAT IS IN THE WORLD"; "THE LOVE OF GOD IS SHED ABROAD IN MY HEART." That is what you call righteous judgment. Righteous judgment is judging yourself in line with the Word of God; judging yourself according to the Word of God, not judging yourself according to what people think, or according to your past life. Whatever God says you are, you are. There- fore, "BEFORE HONOUR IS HUMILITY." "HUMBLE YOUR- SELVES UNDER THE MIGHTY HAND OF GOD, THAT HE MAY EXALT YOU IN DUE TIME." If the pride is still there, you will not be giving many soft answers; you will be a con- tentious person, get agitated and aggravated real easily, and you will be trying to exalt yourself. You will be pushing for- ward for recognition. You will be pushing forward for posi- tion, but the Bible says, Humble yourself under God that He may exalt you in due time. When He has you ready, He will exalt you. Cream always rises to the top.

Be faithful to God, be faithful to His Word, don't be in any hurry. Say, "God, one thing I'm going to be—faithful. Rain, shine, sleet or snow, I'm going to be faithful; I'm going to be loyal to you." Keep staying in that position; humble yourself before God. "God, I'm not moving until you tell me to move." I tell you what, Saints, next thing you know He will exalt you in due time. He will raise you up and have you doing that which He desires you to do. These are some things that Christians today need to learn. We're going to have to be humble people before God, because He says, "BEFORE HONOUR IS HUMILITY." Before God can honor you and me, and lift us up and use us, we are going to have to be the kind of men and women that judge ourselves. Jesus is the Vine, I'm the branch; without Him I can do nothing. But I'm not without Him, I'm with Him. It is not by might, not by power, but it is by the Spirit of God. There is no way you can live the abundant victorious life in your own strength. You don't have it, I don't have it, we can't do it. It is only through the indwelling power of the Holy Spirit of God that you and I can live the abundant life 365 days a year. It is through Jesus Christ that you and I can do all things. It is through Him that we have perfect health. It is through Him we have everything. It is through Him that we are saved, through Him that we were baptized in the Holy Spirit, through Him that we are guided, through Him that we are healed, through Him that we're going to heaven, through Him that we prosper. Jesus said, "IF I BE LIFTED UP I WILL DRAW ALL MEN UNTO ME." As we humble ourselves before God, then God will exalt us and we will be lights in dark places and men and women shall come to know our Lord and Saviour Jesus Christ, because of our lives and our testimony. It is that Spirit that will open our mouths and we will have the boldness of the Lion of Judah, but yet the meekness of the Lamb of God. Jesus was both; He was a Lion and a Lamb. You and I are to be lions, but at the same time we're to be lambs. A lamb is meek, but at the same time the lion is strong. I praise God that Jesus is both of them. For some it is easy to be a lion, but is hard to be a lamb. For some it is easy to be a lamb, but it is hard to be a lion. Praise God, you have the lamb and the lion nature in you, because you have Jesus in you. As we humble ourselves before the Lord, He will exalt us.

VII. OFFENSIVE. Proverbs 18:19, "A BROTHER OFFEND-ED IS HARDER TO BE WON THAN A STRONG CITY: AND THEIR CONTENTIONS ARE LIKE THE BARS OF A CAS-TLE." This truth will keep you from having so much trouble and problems with your brothers and sisters, because you won't be offended any more. If the Word of God offends them, you just love them. You didn't offend them, the Word offended them. Many people say I (Elbert Willis) offended them, but you know how I offended them? I read the Scriptures. A brother offended in his heart is harder to be won than a strong city. I know a brother I offended quite a few years ago. I made many steps to establish a relationship with that man. I went to that man's house one night and right in his house I was making approaches to break down the offense that had been there, and he began to come against me. I just sat there, I just smiled, and God brought to me this Scripture, "A BROTHER OFFENDED IS HARDER TO BE WON THAN A STRONG CITY: AND THEIR CONTENTIONS ARE LIKE THE BARS OF A CASTLE." As you move with God to bring your mind under the control of the Holy Spirit, you want to be careful about offending your brothers and sisters in the Lord. If you offend a brother or sister and they get hard, they are wrong, and that is sin. But at the same time it doesn't justify your sinning by offending.

When I started pastoring 15 years ago, I was pastoring a little church in Central Louisiana. I pastored there 12 or 13 months and God blessed. A lot of people were saved and the church grew, and we built a parsonage right by the church and moved into it. There were three deacons who didn't want the church to be big. When it started getting big they couldn't control it any more. I recognized that this was their problem, but God just began to bless and people began to come in. One Wednesday night at the deacons' meeting, .they got together and put the knife in my back. They turned it, they twisted, and they pulled it out. I had only been serving the Lord for about 15 months, and I blew my cool, I got hot. I didn't say much during the service, but I walked out steaming, and I walked next door to the parsonage and started pulling out furniture and setting it in the front yard. I said, "I'll never leave my furniture in this place another night." For about two hours, while I was steaming, I put the furniture outside. After about two or three hours I cooled off a little bit, and I spent the next two or three hours trying to get the furniture back in the house. The next day I was driving to Oakdale, Louisiana, and God spoke to me and showed me a vision, a piece of paper. I saw the name of one of the deacons at the top of the piece of paper; there was a line down the middle. I knew the man was saved, that he knew Jesus. And God said, "When you can't find more good in them than bad, you have a problem." I thought to myself, wait a minute, God; look what they did to me. God just told me that if I couldn't find more good in them than bad, I had a problem. I turned my car around and started to go back home, and I started praying. If I had known anything about tongues I would have prayed in tongues, but I didn't know anything about tongues. I drove my car back home and God showed me, He said, "Son, I want you to go to every one of those church members' houses and ask them to forgive you for being angry." I said, "Lord, what about their attitudes?" He said, "I am interested in you." So I drove back, and I put the deacons at the end of the list. I started to go to all the houses. I would knock at the door and tell them, "I can't stay long, I have a lot of houses to go to; I've come back to ask you to forgive me for getting angry last night." They'd say, "Brother Willis, you didn't do anything wrong; they did you wrong. They were wrong, they did you dirty." I'd say, "That's not what I came for; I've come to ask you to forgive me because I was angry." I moved 50 mountains into the sea that day. I went to all the houses, and finally only the deacons' homes remained to visit. When I went to those deacons' houses I was hoping they were not there, but they were home. I went to the first one. I said, "Brother, I want you to forgive me for the way I conducted myself last night." He said, "I won't do it." And listen, he was about 60 years of age, like a beanpole, and had his tobacco in his mouth, saying, "No, I won't do it!" I looked at him . . . I said, "Well, OK." God was performing surgery, on me! I went to the next deacon's house and asked him to forgive me. He said, "No." After I obeyed and went to those deacons' houses, I got in my car, and the peace of God hit me. They were both wrong; I asked them to forgive me, they wouldn't forgive me, even though they had done me wrong. But two wrongs don't make a right. Ever since then, I have this principle: Any time I can't find more good than bad, I ask God to forgive me, especially if they are a Christian. This will help you to love others, even if they have done you wrong. This helps me not to have an attitude in my own life that would cause offense. I still walk that way. I will not allow hate and resentment in my heart against anybody, regardless of what has been done. Does it come? Sure it comes. I have the right to refuse that package. Resentment and bitterness will sever your spiritual relationship between you and Jesus. Learn now these words of wisdom, and it will save you a lot of trouble in the future.

VIII. STABILITY. Proverbs 16:3, "COMMIT THY WORKS UNTO THE LORD, AND THY THOUGHTS SHALL BE ESTABLISHED." If you can't commit your works unto God then your thoughts will not be established. Any time you're shaky, then your mind is not under the control of the Word of God. Any time there is confusion or frustration, disappointment, discouragement, doubt, and worry, you need to realize you have not committed your works unto the Lord, and therefore your thoughts are not established. You are not stable in God; your mind is not renewed by the Word of God; so you must make sure that everything you do is committed unto the Lord. Keep your thoughts upon Jesus; keep your mind upon God. Make sure that you are doing everything as unto the Lord. "SEEK YE FIRST THE KINGDOM OF GOD, AND HIS RIGHTEOUSNESS; AND ALL THESE THINGS SHALL BE ADDED UNTO YOU." (Matthew 6:33)

IX. PERCEPTION. Proverbs 16:2 says, "ALL THE WAYS OF A MAN ARE CLEAN IN HIS OWN EYES." Here you have to admit to yourself that not everything you do is good. The only way you can really accept that something you're doing is not right, is that the Holy Spirit will show you. The Holy Spirit has to prick your conscience. You think it is all right; you always think it is right, unless God through His Word and by His Spirit shows you it is wrong. This is why many people's minds cannot be renewed today. They don't know enough of the Word; they don't have their mind renewed by the Word enough to know what is wrong with their lives. They think everything is all right, but they are blind. I'm speaking to me as well. The only way I've ever seen what was wrong in my life was when the Holy Spirit of God, through some teaching, or cassette, or book, or directly speaking to me, revealed to me what was wrong; otherwise, I thought everything was all right. When I started preaching 15 years ago, I didn't think there was very much wrong with me; I was doing a good job. Two years after, I was baptized in the Holy Ghost and I realized everything was haywire. The Holy Spirit began to make it real to me.

Many people don't really want to see themselves as God sees them. If you let God unfold you, believe me, He will pull the covers back. For your mind to be renewed by the Word of God, you have to let the Lord pull the covers back. Realize this perception, and realize you can't do it naturally. Here is a mistake a lot of people are making: they are trying to examine themselves. You are foolish if you try to examine yourself; you will always find yourself right. It will be your husband who is wrong, or your wife, or your neighbor, or your boss. It is not going to be you. The reason why you're not doing better than you are is your boss' fault. You ladies say it is your husband—if he wouldn't be so mean, everything would be all right. You men say you would be doing so much better if you had the right kind of wife. The real problem is SELF. The only one Who can help you to see what is wrong is God. I praise Him for it. No one would ever have made me believe the things that were wrong with me that God revealed to me. My wife tried to tell me some of them, but she didn't know what she was talking about. I tried to tell my wife some things that were wrong with her, and she thought I was picking on her. "ALL THE WAYS OF A MAN ARE CLEAN IN HIS OWN EYES." Say, "Father, in the Name of Jesus, expose me." Don't worry about your wife, don't worry about your husband; God can clean you up and then get your mate. You become the vessel. Men, don't worry about promotions; let God clean you up and you will get the promotion.

X. A SNARE. Proverbs 29:25 says, "THE FEAR OF MAN BRINGETH A SNARE." How would you tell your boss that you don't need "Blue Cross" any more? He's got you snared. "I believe in speaking in tongues." Why don't you tell everybody? Fear of whom? Not fear of God. Are you afraid of the devil? Fear of man bringeth a snare. It traps you and holds you. Do you know why Christians are not brighter lights than they are? Guess why they don't witness more? Fear of what people might say about them. They camouflage and say, "Well, I'm going to witness in wisdom." You know why a lot of times you don't get free in praising God? Fear of what somebody might say. Fear of man brings snares. As long as the devil can use fear of people on you, you will never be mighty with God. This is the yoke of all yokes that must be broken. It will keep your mind from being renewed. These are some words of wisdom for you.

XI. FLATTERY. Proverbs 28:23, "HE THAT REBUKETH A MAN AFTERWARDS SHALL FIND MORE FAVOR THAN HE THAT FLATTERETH WITH THE TONGUE." Complimenting people is all right, but you better make sure it is not a habit pattern that you have inherited from the world. You know what the world teaches you? Compliment people. You know what the world teaches men in high offices and jobs? You know how you get work out of your people? Feed their ego. Find something to compliment them for. We want to say good things, but don't go around flattering. You are meeting so many people, and you've been trained by the world to flatter them, until when you get around them you have to flatter them or you don't have anything to say; and you feel lost if you don't have anything to say. The world always has something to say. "Boy, that's sure a nice dress." "I like the way your hair is fixed; I like those shoes; I like that shirt; I like that tie." It's all right if you like it, but you better make sure it is honest. You better make sure it is not a habit pattern developed within you. Compliments are real and they are good, but the system of the world is built on flattery. If a man is working on the job and he makes five mistakes and does something right twice, be sure and compliment the two; if you don't, you are going to destroy him. When I was in the world, I was in management. I managed a multi-million dollar finance company. Just say what the Word says: "HE THAT IS IN YOU IS GREATER THAN HE THAT IS IN THE WORLD." That's not flattering, just the truth. "You can do all things through Jesus Christ, Who strengthens you." That just tells you what God's Word says. " . . . FIND MORE FAVOR THAN HE THAT FLATTERETH WITH THE TONGUE." Most Christians never think about things like this.

Let me share this with the ladies. Ladies are good about complimenting each other, and they'll say, "Your hair looks nice," and then walk off and say something else. I know men do it too, ladies. But somehow or other you're just a little stronger in this area. That is your mountain. Men have some mountains to climb, too. Men are not as quick to flatter, but women are quick to flatter. "Oh! That picture is so beautiful." It is good if it is, but don't walk off and think something else; if you do, you just lied. And you are interfering with coming to the place of the conquest, conquering of the mind. There is a place for good, sincere, honest compliments. The Bible will compliment you. "YOU CAN DO ALL THINGS THROUGH JESUS CHRIST." He says, "YOU ARE A SON OF GOD"; that's a compliment. "YOU ARE BORN OF GOD." "HE THAT IS IN YOU IS GREATER THAN HE THAT IS IN THE WORLD." There is a place for compliments. "HE THAT REBUKETH A MAN AFTERWARDS SHALL FIND MORE FAVOR THAN HE THAT FLATTERETH WITH THE TONGUE." Just make sure, as you face people on your job, at home, when you tell them you love them, you tell them you appreciate them, make sure that you're not operating in flattery. The whole system of our world is a flattering system. You can flatter people and really not mean to be dishonest, thinking you are helping them. If you can't say something honestly, just don't say anything. Really, why do you have to say something? I know you've been taught all your life that you have to find something good to say about somebody. If you can say it honestly, say it; if you can't, just say, "Glory to God, I believe the Word of God to be the Truth." Then you are saying good things, not flattering anyone. Magnify the Lord, it's a lot better talk.

XII. **PROMOTION.** Psalm 75:6-7 says, "PROMOTION COMETH NEITHER FROM THE EAST, NOR FROM THE WEST, NOR FROM THE SOUTH. BUT GOD IS THE JUDGE: HE PUTTETH DOWN ONE, AND SETTETH UP ANOTHER." nuggets I've learned in hours of study, so that you can get the same truths I have, and use them in your Christian life. promotion comes from God, and the boss is the channel. You don't have to tell him that, but you need to be smart enough to realize it. If you're looking to a man to promote you, then that man can promote you. That man also can put you down, but if God promotes you, not even the boss can put you down. When it looks like he's going to put you down, God puts you back up in a greater position. You are respected, the Bible tells you that. The Bible tells you to treat him right, give him a good day's work. You do right, you treat the boss right, give him his rightful position because he is the boss; but be smart enough to know that you are being promoted, you are getting blessed, because you are faithful to the Almighty God. That is where promotion comes from; it comes from God. This will help you to do a better job, because the Bible says do it as unto the Lord. Ladies, do your housework as unto the Lord. Do your housework as if the next visitor was going to be Jesus, because, ladies, He's living there in your house. I hope He's not living in a mess. The Scriptures say do everything as unto the Lord. And men, if you do all your work as unto the Lord, you can't help but get rich. But if you don't, you're going to hinder God from promoting you and next thing you know you will blame it on your boss. All the employers in the world can't keep a man or a woman who is faithful to God from maturing, and growing, and prospering. You must be faithful to God. You'll have to know that God is the one

Who promotes. It doesn't come from the east, or the west, or the south, but God is the judge. You can't be slothful on the job and slothful at home, and then turn around and be diligent with God. Slothfulness shows up in everything you do. You show me a man or a woman who is not diligent at home; I'll show you a man or woman who will never be really successful with God. I don't care how it looks or how it appears; they may look right now like they're climbing high but after a while a lot of others will pass them by, because God is the judge. Be faithful in all things, and God Himself will promote you.

XIII. KNOWLEDGE. I Corinthians 8:16 says, "KNOWLEDGE PUFFETH UP, BUT LOVE EDIFIETH." Here we are teaching you to study and get knowledge of the Bible, and yet the Scripture says it puffs up. You can get Bible knowledge and get puffed up. You can begin to learn so many of the principles and truths of God, and get puffed up because of your knowledge. Any man or woman who gets a lot of knowledge in any area, unless they allow God to deal with them, they are prideful. It is so in carpentry, plumbing, engineering, any natural field. Promotions come, recognition comes, success comes, prosperity comes; if that man doesn't let Jesus do a work in his life he will get puffed up. It is a principle. A preacher can be faithful and diligent to God and learn the Word of God, and study the Word of God; a preacher can do that and get puffed up. No one is excluded; just because you're a preacher, it doesn't exclude you from sin. So guard against it.

As you begin to learn the Word of God and the things of God, God is going to begin to prosper you. You can learn the Word of God where you know that no man can keep you down, but if you're not careful, even that knowledge can puff you up. I know that no man can keep me from being successful. Everybody in the world can't keep me from being successful. Only one can do it—that's me. If I'm faithful to God and obey His Word, you can think what you want to think, do what you want to do, but as I am faithful to God and obey Him, He is going to bless me. That same knowledge can cause you to get puffed up.

XIV. **TALKING.** Talking can keep me from conquering my mind? You can be assured it will. Proverbs 10:19, "IN THE MULTITUDE OF WORDS THERE WANTETH NOT SIN: BUT HE THAT REFRAINETH HIS LIPS IS WISE." There is no way in the world that we can talk a lot without sinning. Any time you get into a fellowship and you spend two or three hours together (a group of you fellowshipping), somewhere somebody lied or exaggerated, or stretched the truth. The other people don't know, but you know. The Holy Spirit told you about it, and you thought, "Oh, I wish I hadn't said that." "All the ways are clean in your own eyes." The Bible says, "IN THE MULTITUDE OF WORDS THERE WANTETH NOT SIN." You can't get together with fellowship parties and not sin. Brother Willis, what do we do? Don't do much of it. Spend your time fellowshipping with God. Don't talk contrary to the Bible when you talk to God, talk Bible. Most people spend a lot of time praying and talking to God and they sin in the multitude of their words while they are praying. "God, I want you to do all you can with my husband, you know how hard and stubborn he is." You have already talked too much. Only speak those words that edify and minister grace unto those who hear. You are not ministering grace when you tell Him junk like that; He knows your husband. "IN THE MULTITUDE OF WORDS THERE WANTETH NOT SIN; BUT HE THAT REFRAINETH HIS LIPS IS WISE." This is one of the most difficult areas there is.

When I was a Baptist pastor, you know what my brag was? Every month I was in every home. I had my little card system set up, and every month I visited everybody's home. And "IN THE MULTITUDE OF WORDS THERE WANTETH NOT SIN." Whether they wanted me or not, I was there. "BUT HE THAT REFRAINETH HIS LIPS IS WISE." The hardest mountain I had to climb was when I began to cut out the fellowship. Just to stay by yourself and study the Word and pray, you know that's really a tough thing to do? If you think it's not, why don't you take a night and just go in your bedroom at 7 o'clock; don't turn the TV on, go in there and stay, just you and God, until 10 o'clock. If you're not used to doing it, you'll be in a struggle; you'll walk out of there fifty times. You will be fidgety, you will be looking for someone to talk to. Do you know that most people can't stay one whole day all by themselves? After a few hours they are ready to climb the walls. Learn to keep your talking according to the Word of God.

XV. **BEING USEABLE.** Matthew 20:26-28 says, "BUT WHOSOEVER WILL BE GREAT AMONG YOU (you want to be great in the kingdom of God? God wants you to be), LET HIM BE YOUR MINISTER; AND WHOSOEVER WILL BE CHIEF AMONG YOU, LET HIM BE YOUR SERVANT; EVEN AS THE SON OF MAN CAME NOT TO BE MINISTERED UNTO, BUT TO MINISTER, AND TO GIVE HIS LIFE A RANSOM FOR MANY." Are you really willing to give up your life, your ways? Are you really willing to give up all that fellowship time, and give up your dreams, aspirations, and give your life up? Are you willing to lay aside the things of the world and give your life to God, and the Word of God, and be sober minded and walk with God? If you want to be great, be a servant. I put in more hours, I'm sure, in studying and preparing a teaching or sermon, than many men do in a job. I have to serve the body of Christ; that's my ministry to serve you. When you read the pages of this book, I desire to serve you something to eat. You can't spend eight, ten or twelve hours a day studying the Word. So you are out there doing what God wants you to do and I have to be doing what God wants me to do, so when you pick up this book, I can say, let's look at the Word of God. So I can share with you the nuggets I've learned in hours of study, so that you can get the same truths I have, and use them in your Christian life. "BUT WHOSOEVER WILL BE GREAT AMONG YOU, LET HIM BE YOUR SERVANT; EVEN AS THE SON OF MAN CAME NOT TO BE MINISTERED UNTO (we are going to have to come to the place where you and I can be ministered unto), BUT TO MINISTER." Are you willing to give up enough, so you can learn enough of the Word of God so you don't have to be ministered unto, so that you can be able to minister? That's what Jesus, the Son of God, came to do— to minister. God wants every one of you to be ministering out there in your neighborhood, on your job, at school, wherever you are.

XVI. **FUTILITY OF HUMAN EFFORT TO PRODUCE ANY SPIRITUAL RESULTS.** The only way spiritual results come about is by God moving in your life and mine. That's spiritual results, and that is lasting results. Let me just give you an example to help you realize it. In salesmanship in the world, they bring the men in for pep talks. They use their system to challenge them and pump them up and keep the goals before them. And they do it week after week after week, because it doesn't last very long. The Word of God is the only thing that will give you spiritual life. All your natural straining won't help. It won't heal your sore toe. It takes the Spirit of God and the Word of God. All human effort is futile to a brain to force spiritual results. As you and I yield to the Holy Spirit of God we become vessels for God to flow through to bring forth spiritual results, but it is not the work of human effort. People get saved, baptized, and healed all the time. I lay my hands on people week after week all around the country, and see them get healed. There is still no human effort in it. I'm a vessel, I'm obeying God, I'm laying my hands, I'm speaking it. The only One Who can heal them is Jesus Christ, the Son of the living God. I can speak the Word and teach the Word and put it into print. I prepare, I study, I work on it, I know it, I bring it to you, I'm diligent about it. But the only thing that will be lasting will be what the Spirit of God does in your life through the words spoken or written. I can challenge you, but if the Holy Spirit doesn't make it real to you, it will not last. It will just be for a season. The futility of all human effort. "NOT I LIVE, BUT CHRIST LIVES IN ME." "Jesus is the Vine; I'm the branch. Without Him I can't do anything." The vine and the branch. The branch draws everything it needs from the vine. My arm is a branch

133

from this body. Everything this branch (my arm) needs, it has to draw from this body. Cut this branch from this body, and it withers, it dies, it has no power. This arm cannot move, it has no strength, disconnected from this body, but connected to this body I can do many things with this arm. You and I are connected to Jesus; we can do all things. Disconnected from Jesus we cannot produce anything.

I believe the Word of God is going to begin to work in your life like it never has before. I believe that your mind is going to begin to be renewed like it never has been before, and you are going to begin to hear God speak to you and lead you and guide you like never before. Just ask the Holy Spirit of God to do a new work in you. Jesus said in John 16:13 that the Spirit came to guide me into all truth. Ask the Spirit to begin to guide you into truth about yourself, the corrections that need to be made in your personal life. Realize that the conquest of your mind is an absolute necessity to moving into the greater things of God. Begin today to open your entire life to the ministry of the Spirit of God, and He will begin the conforming of your being to the image of the Son of the Living God.

NOTE:

An eight tape series on the Conquest of the mind, by Elbert Willis, is available from FILL THE GAP PUBLICATION, P.O. Box 30760, Lafayette, La. 70503.

The series comes complete in a vinyl cassette album, with outlines for study. TOTAL PRICE - $20.00.